A TIME TO WRITE

Other books by Loula Grace Erdman

ANOTHER SPRING

A WONDERFUL THING AND OTHER STORIES

LIFE WAS SIMPLER THEN

ROOM TO GROW

THE MAN WHO TOLD THE TRUTH

MANY A VOYAGE

THE GOOD LAND

THE SHORT SUMMER

THE WIDE HORIZON

THE FAR JOURNEY

THREE AT THE WEDDING

THE WIND BLOWS FREE

THE EDGE OF TIME

LONELY PASSAGE

THE YEARS OF THE LOCUST

A Time to Write

Loula Grace Erdman

DODD, MEAD & COMPANY
NEW YORK

Library of Congress Catalog Card Number: 69-18463

Printed in the United States of America

For Phelps Platt, who urged me to write this book
and
For Margaret Norton, who helped me bring it through

A TIME TO WRITE

Chapter One

Kansas City, Missouri, has always been justifiably proud of its Union Station. For one thing, it was exceeded in size only by New York's Grand Central and the Pennsylvania Terminal. Trains with romantic names like Super Chief and Southern Belle and Portland Rose rolled in, proud as any ocean Queen dropping anchor. People still point out the bullet scars on the front entrance—reminders of the battle Pretty Boy Floyd and his buddies fought with policemen in an attempt to free the bank robber, Frank Nash. Four policemen and Nash were killed before it was over. Another story, no less colorful but with a happier ending, is told about the time a few dozen wild steers escaped from a freight car and stampeded up into the terminal. A station attendant bulldogged one of them in the ladies' room and soon order was restored.

For the most part though, it is much like any other large union station from New York to California. There are the usual restaurants, shops, newsstands and drugstores. The usual doors open to admit incoming passengers or to send outward bound ones on their way. There are rows of seats occupied by travelers wearing the curiously detached look peculiar to displaced persons. It is not, however, a likely place in which to begin a writing career.

Even so, that is where mine started once upon a New Year's Eve.

I had spent Christmas vacation with my parents in Missouri and was on my way back to Amarillo, Texas, where I taught in junior high school. A storm had blazed across the midwest, delaying the Santa Fe Chief. I discovered that instead of the usual hour's wait between trains I would probably be in Kansas City for six hours or more.

Ordinarily I would have telephoned some of my many friends or relatives in the city suggesting they join me, or better still, I join them until such time as my train would arrive. But the storm made this impractical; no one would ask his worst enemy to come out on an evening like this. Instead, I ate dinner alone. When I had finished, I bought some magazines and settled down to read. Soon I had gone through them and turned to people watching. Before long I discarded that also. Most of the interesting specimens seemed to have stayed home this evening. I went back to the newsstand to look for a fresh supply of magazines.

And there I saw it—a notebook such as school children use. Beside it, an ordinary pencil, nicely sharpened. I cleared my throat. "I'll take it," I said, pointing to the notebook. "And it," indicating the pencil. Even to my own ears I sounded sinister. As if maybe I meant to use the pencil to puncture someone's jugular vein, and, once the foul deed was accomplished, wrap the bloody remains in the notebook pages.

I told myself I was going to write a letter. But all the time I knew better. I was going to write a short story.

Later I was to discover that most writers start in secret and with something very like apology. If questioned, they will probably deny the fact that they are writing, like children caught in some grave fault. By and by they may become compulsive talkers about the work in progress, but rarely is this true in the beginning.

The idea of writing was not a new one with me. At the age of eight or so I had scrawled out a story in longhand and sent it to our county paper, the Higginsville *Advance*. The editor, a good friend of my father's, returned it with a kindly note of rejection. I still have his letter. He told me I showed promise and I should by all means keep on trying, but at the present he was unable to use my story. Years later when I was in high school, he published a poem of mine on the front page of the paper—a triumph which made me a bit difficult to live with for a few days. Family and friends soon cut me down to size, however, and after that I decided, as many writers before and since have done, that I would be a one appearance author and let my reputation stand on that single offering.

But here I was, writing once more.

I took the notebook and pencil to a desk in the women's waiting room (no stampeding steers there this evening and scarcely any women) and began putting words down. Just like that. A scene of a short story, something that could happen to someone I knew. I set it in Missouri, a place also familiar to me.

After all the years between, that is still the way I write. I put down what comes to me, with no specific thought as to whether it is the beginning, the middle, or the end. When an idea hits, I grab a pencil and jot it down, or go to my typewriter. Later I sort out material, organize, write proper beginnings and ends, make clear transitions. I fill in, enlarge or condense as the case seems to warrant. Always in the beginning, however, a story starts with a character and how he would react in some given situation. I know there are those who lean to outlines and insist the writer should know clearly, before setting down a single word, exactly what he means to do in the piece of writing he is about to undertake. I have no quarrel with them or with any other method employed by anyone. Writing is as individual as getting religion or falling in love and everyone must approach it in his own way.

I still believe, however, that it is important to set down a thought when it comes. I urge my students to do the same, illustrating my point with the story about the author who had such a wonderful idea he fell on his knees to thank God for it. When he got up, he had forgotten what it was.

"Write it down first," I insist. "Then thank God afterwards."

Through the years I have practiced what I preached.

I have used church programs for this purpose, and backs of envelopes and scraps of paper and even, upon occasion, a paper napkin. In working on this manuscript I have repeatedly come across notes I made while writing previous books. I look at them and wonder why I wrote some of these scrawls that confront me. Where was I? What prompted the thoughts which now seem alien and strange? It is like encountering a ghost of one's former self. So Scrooge must have felt when he saw the Ghost of Christmas Past.

At any rate, that was the premise on which I began my first

story, there in the Union Station at Kansas City—that I must write what came to me, when it came.

Eventually the train pulled in and I boarded it, clutching my notebook with some ten or twelve pages filled.

It never occurred to me to take a Pullman. On a teacher's salary? Don't be silly. Besides, a friend had taught me a good trick about night train travel. Select a coach with few people in it, not a difficult feat in those depression years, and settle yourself and your luggage in two outside seats facing each other. If you use exactly the right skill in disarranging your belongings, people will pass by rather than bother you. I believe those old coaches are no longer in use, but at that time it was possible to pull out a footrest, remove the cushion from the window seat and place it on the extension thus provided. This, together with the facing seats, forms an adequate bed if you are young enough and tired enough. If you have a taste for luxury, you could rent a pillow from the news vendor. Your coat is as good a cover as anyone could want. Kick off your shoes, unfasten any hooks that jab, and settle down for a night's sleep, lulled by the knowledge of how much you are saving. The idea! you rationalize, of spending all that money on a Pullman when you are every bit as comfortable where you are.

Tonight luck was with me. Only a few people were on the coach I had chosen, all of whom seemed to be traveling on passes. I had the feeling the conductor was considering rolling out the red carpet for me, his one paying passenger. I knew I would have no trouble with him about the disarrangement of the seats. The lights went off early. I stretched out on my improvised Pullman and prepared for what I thought was going to be a good night's rest.

Only that's not the way things turned out at all. My heroine gave me no rest, not for one moment. She stood beside me, real as one of my best friends. She engaged in brilliant conversation which I wanted to set down, but there was no light to write by. She went about manifold activities such as going downtown to shop and getting into, and out of, various scrapes. In fact, not only did she spend an active night but she would not allow me to sleep either.

I found out for myself a fact that many writers before and since have discovered. Writing at night is not always satisfactory. You are more than likely to lie awake, once you are in bed, staring at the ceiling, trying to get your characters into or out of difficulties. Since much of my writing has of necessity been done in the evening, I have tried to meet this problem by finishing a chapter, or a division of a chapter, or even a scene, before going to bed.

Some there are who do not subscribe to this method, preferring rather to leave a few loose ends hanging in order that they may pick them up the next day. But for me, my own way seems to work best. That, of course, I did not know at the time I was writing my first story.

I was quite ready to get up the next morning when signs of daylight began to show. I unmade my berth, putting the misplaced cushion back in place and pushing in the footrest. I took out my notebook and began trying to set down the things my heroine had said and done during the night. Of course, this was impossible to achieve. A story may be a sort of daydream flowing pleasantly along like a vision brought on by a whiff of opium. The mere act of picking up a pencil and pushing it across the page tends to put the dream to rout. But on the other hand, the act of holding the pencil furnishes an excellent compensation. It sets your mind to work, which is a good way to harness a dream.

Soon I was putting words down once more. Not with the ease and smoothness they had marched through my mind during the night, but nevertheless I was getting them down. I wrote most of the morning. Before the conductor called "Amarillo," I had written the ending.

At that time I was staying with my sister and brother-in-law. They, with their young son, met me at the train. My first words, almost before the greetings were finished, were, "Do you know where I can rent a typewriter?"

My brother-in-law, a lawyer, said there was no need to rent one; he had an extra typewriter at his office. The next evening when he came home he brought it with him.

I have seen and used many typewriters since then, but I have never encountered one exactly like this. It was squat and pudgy, a dull black in color, like Queen Victoria in her widow's weeds. One of the keys—the letter C—was twisted slightly so that it stuck. Each time I struck it, I had to reach up and release it by hand. Not without a struggle did it come loose. Like a cat in a tree, it apparently found ascent easy, descent impossible. In all honesty I must admit, however, it never failed to respond to the second try.

Not only did that typewriter look and act strangely, it sounded like no piece of machinery I had ever heard before or since. The keys did not rattle; they clanged, making a sullen roar, a hopeless, damned sound. I named it Callie (short for calliope), and on it I learned to type. That is, I learned after my fashion, a method I termed the Hit-and-Hope system. (Hit a key and hope it's the right one.) I used two fingers; I watched the keyboard as I typed; I kept my copy on the left instead of the right side. I did everything exactly wrong; but even so, I continued to put words on paper.

And finally I finished typing my story.

By that time it was the first of February. To me, this is a nondescript month, too early to think overmuch of spring, and winter is growing grey around the temples and beginning to sag all over. After one gets past the age of valentines, there's just not much to February.

I was still going by dead reckoning as it were, with no help from anyone. I did not even know there were such things as writers' magazines or books on writing. I knew only there were magazines which published short stories people wrote. Heretofore I had been on the receiving end of the line of this procedure. Now I was a producer.

My brother-in-law subscribed to the *Saturday Evening Post*. Ah, I thought, that's where I'll send my story. Again, I did things all the wrong way. I folded my manuscript as I would have done a business letter and mailed it in a legal size envelope. It never occurred to me that I needed a carbon. I did, however, have some dim knowledge or caution or natural courtesy which told me to enclose return postage. Not that I thought for one moment it would be needed. This done, I dropped the envelope into the mails and waited.

A peculiar and special glow comes to an author who has just mailed off a manuscript—a feeling that is intensified if he keeps the knowledge to himself. It is a mixture of complacency, superiority, excitement and smugness. By and by, when one's ears have been beaten down often enough, when one's vanity has had a permanent crimp, when one's ego has been thoroughly trampled, this glow is considerably dimmed.

But it is never lost entirely. If it were, few people would continue writing.

For ten rich, full days the glow lasted. When I came home from school on the eleventh day, I found a fat envelope, legal size, with my name typed across it. I still think there is some twisted sort of justice back of the rule which says an author must enclose a stamped, self-addressed envelope with his manuscript. It is like signing one's own doom. It is like being made to break off the switch which Mama will use on you. I took one long, sinking look at my name, typed in Callie's inimitable style, the C in Grace showing plainly it had needed two licks to make it function. I went to my room, there to open without witnesses the envelope which had put to an end my ten days' dream. I drew out the letter clipped to the first page. Perhaps the editor wanted to suggest revisions.

The editor wished to do nothing more than to tell me he regretted my story did not meet the requirements of the *Post*. His regrets were formal, routine, and as impersonal as a road map. Even I, unaccustomed to such things, knew it for what it was—a form rejection slip, the likes of which, I suspected, were going up and down the land blasting the hopes of would-be writers like myself.

I shrank back instinctively as if I had been discovered in some sneaking crime which was not only petty but despicable and maybe even a little ridiculous. A crime with no dignity, with no real excuse for being. I stuffed the returned story, together with the form rejection, into a drawer of my desk and pulled some papers over it. At that moment, my sister called, "Dinner's ready."

"You look funny," she said as I took my place at the table. "What's wrong? You sick or something?"

I said, "Nothing—nothing. I feel fine."

Immediately I began to be very gay and eat too fast and overmuch.

My sister, who has a great wisdom and inner vision, asked, "Have you heard anything from your story?" (Of course she had seen the envelope when she took the mail from the box. The question was academic).

"It came back," I said hollowly.

In the years that have followed I have wished hundreds of times I could say of a returned manuscript, "Well, it's back," making the announcement with proper nonchalance and the exactly correct degree of lightness. This I have never learned to do. I seriously doubt that any writer has completely mastered the technique. My first impulse is to hide the rejection, even from myself. I skim quickly through the letter or slip accompanying the manuscript. It may be several hours, perhaps even a full day, before I can force myself to go back and reread it.

Now that the secret was out I felt better. I stopped eating immediately.

"You shouldn't have sent it to the *Post* in the first place," my sister told me.

In that single sentence she uttered one of the most profound bits of advice anyone can offer a beginning writer. I looked at her in amazement. I, who had felt so smart at having written a story, did not possess the greater wisdom she exhibited. My story was simply not *Post* caliber. I could see that now and, seeing, I felt some of the hurt and the sting of rejection leaving me. Why should I send my fledgling out to fly with the eagles? It was not fair to the story or the author.

"I'll never do it again," I promised.

For the most part, I have kept my word. I make an honest attempt to study the magazine before I offer it a piece of my writing. That does not mean I ceased to have rejections; but at least, I received them from magazines whose editorial policy seemed somewhat akin to the nature of the material I sent. This, I am told, is not always the practice of authors, especially beginners. Stories have been sent to magazines that have ceased publishing months before. I once heard of a writer who offered an article on "How to Choose Your Family Doctor" to the *Christian Science Monitor*. One of the first lessons a beginner should learn is the necessity to study markets.

February slid into March and March went the way of all months, as did April. My story still lay in the bottom drawer of my desk, covered now by an increasing accumulation of papers and so on. In May, I began a systematic cleaning of my room preparatory to going to Missouri for the summer. In the process I found the story at the bottom of the pile. I looked at it thoughtfully. "Well, you gave up pretty quickly on that one, didn't you," I told myself.

I smoothed out the pages and decided the typing was poor. And folding a manuscript did seem a bit sloppy. Perhaps it was better to mail it flat.

I went to a stationery shop to buy envelopes. "The size to hold typing paper," I specified. In the purchase I did have some foretaste of knowledge, some intuitive wisdom which would serve me well in years to come. I bought six envelopes, taking it for granted I would need them.

I did. I retyped my story and sent it off. It came back. I repeated the process. Back it came again. I used up a third set of envelopes and, in due season, had the lot of them returned.

That summer I went to school, an activity scarcely conducive to writing of a creative nature. Just at the end of the term, something happened which was to change the course of my writing life. In the college bookstore I saw a copy of a writer's magazine. I bought it and rushed back to my room, threw myself across my bed and began to read.

I was wise enough to discard the bright promises of the ads. But the articles—they were another thing again. Why hadn't I known such magazines existed, slanted toward people like me? Those who wanted to write. An item under the heading, "Current Markets," made me sit up straight. The editor of a small magazine published in Kansas City was asking for stories. "By beginners," he specified, "because our rates are low."

Kansas City, the scene of my story. Beginners, which I most certainly was. Obviously, the editor was addressing himself directly to me. The magazine, tucked into the current envelope holding my story, went back with me to Amarillo when I returned for the opening of school. As soon as the usual routine matters were taken care of, I mailed the story to the editor.

That was a busy fall for me. I scarcely had time to think about my story, which was all to the good. It didn't come back and it didn't come back.

For some reason I cannot for the life of me remember now, I decided not to go to Missouri for Christmas. A strange decision, viewed in retrospect, for we are a family people, given to gatherings at any holiday time and most especially

at Christmas. Perhaps I wanted to stay in Texas and watch
young nephew Bobby's reaction to the season.

But even the child's enthusiasm seemed flat. I set up the
crèche with his help, relating the old, old story as we put the
various pieces into place. "And the shepherds saw the Star
and they went to the manger," I said. Then, as we set the
Wise Men into position, I continued, "And the Wise Men
saw the Star and they went, too."

He had stood it as long as he could. "Did you go, too?" he
asked anxiously, evidently unwilling to have me miss anything really worth seeing.

At the moment I felt as old as time; as if I, too, might have
made that long gone journey. "It's no good, not going home
for Christmas," I told myself. "I'll never do things this way
again." (Later, I was to write a short story about going home
for Christmas. It was titled, "The Rabbit's Tale Was Square";
and some there are who maintain it's the best thing I ever
did. It could well be. I knew exactly, from experience, how
my various characters were feeling at the time I was writing
about them.)

Christmas Eve day came. The mail brought cards which I
opened only to find that Christmas cards, in which I most especially delight, had lost some of their flavor. Among them
was a brown Manila envelope whose contour (and contents)
were by now thoroughly familiar to me. This I waited to
open until last, since I already knew what was in it. Sure
enough, there was my story with the usual form rejection
attached. I put it aside and reread my cards.

This done, I collected the lot of them and went back to my
room. I reached for the story in order to put it into the
familiar niche in the bottom desk drawer. As I did so, I saw

some writing on the back of the rejection slip. I turned it over to read, and then such a yell broke from my lips that the family came on the run to see if by any chance my mail had yielded a bomb or a scorpion. I stood still, holding out the slip with its written message.

"He wants a revision," I said.

No need to say who, or what.

Sure enough, on the back of the rejection slip was a short cryptic note, the burden of which was that if I were willing to revise the story, the editor would pay me fifteen dollars for it. I was to shorten and I was to omit a certain scene which he designated. It so happened this was the one I had written first, the one which had started the story.

Many times since I have found I must take this same action —omit the scene which had suggested the story in the first place. I have come to think of the initial idea as bearing the same relation to a story that a diving board does to a swimmer. The board furnishes the spring necessary to plunge the swimmer into the pool. After he's in the water, he is on his own. Once the writer is into his story, he may find himself getting farther and farther away from his original idea.

At the time, however, I had no such wisdom. I had been asked to cut out a scene, and that was what I meant to do. I worked the rest of the day. I shortened. I tightened. I left out the scene to which the editor had specifically objected. I retyped the story. Callie behaved nobly. Once or twice the C almost went down on the first lick. That afternoon, late, I had the story in the mails.

It was about the sixth of January when a letter came from the editor. He said the revision was not quite up to what he had expected, but even so he would buy the story. He paid on publication.

I sat there, looking at the letter. (I still have it.) That beautiful, glorious letter telling me an editor was willing to pay for something I had written. It was my promissory note to triumph. I read it again. Then I went out, very quietly (now I know I was in a kind of daze) and broke the news to my sister. I must have been in a state of shock, for I do not in the least remember what her reactions were.

Even though I had sold one story, I was still flying blind as it were. Beyond the magazine I had discovered the summer before, I had read nothing calculated to help me in writing. I had never been to a writers' conference or enrolled in a writing class. I was writing much as someone plays a musical instrument by ear.

I was doing what I suspect most beginning writers do. Paraphrasing the stories I had read and liked. Again, as is the case with most beginners, I colored them with my own experiences and imagination. All I really knew about a story was that it concerned people and it was short. I never bothered to count words. I usually ran out of something to say and stopped with seventeen pages or so, which was all to the good.

I could not, as so many writers declare is their method, have a "set time and a place to write." I wrote when and where I could. After all my other duties were finished, I wrote. It is a practice I continue, even now. I get everything else out of the way and then settle down to writing. Only, it seems I could not then, nor can I now, stay settled long. The telephone rings and friends drop by, and various things happen to keep me away from my typewriter. But then, as now, I kept at it. Before I knew it the last of May had come and I was packing to go to Missouri for the summer. I tucked Callie into my trunk.

"Don't you know," friends warned me, "an upright typewriter isn't supposed to be shipped through in a trunk! You'll ruin it."

I went right on packing. The next day I was off and gone, Callie inside my trunk, checked through on my ticket. Once I was home, I lifted the typewriter out, set it on a strong bridge table in my room, untangled a few keys, inserted a sheet of paper and started writing. Off the typewriter went, smooth as a whistle. Of course, though, the C still stuck.

From the window of my upstairs bedroom I looked out across a garden bordered by an orchard with fields coming to its edge. Beyond the fields, the tight, snug well-built houses of friends and kin and neighbors. The Missouri farm country, my heritage. My own ancestors had been a part of this region, had carved out its roads and helped build its schools and settled its towns. They had gone to its weddings and christenings and funerals. They had tilled the soil and run the stores and attended the churches. Some of them lay buried in its cemeteries.

I was heir to the stories of the small and intimate details of their lives and to the tales of their heartaches and despairs and frustrations as well. I knew the roads these people traveled as they went about their daily affairs. The slope of the fields. The way the streams meandered in and out. The blush of roadside roses in summer and the crimson of sumac in the fall. Even so, since I had been brought up here, I think I took it all pretty much for granted.

Our farm was a part of the original homestead. My father,

his father, and his grandfather had lived in the family home which was set back from the road a quarter of a mile or so, which was the approved site for Missouri houses in the earlier days of the state's history. My father brought my mother home as a bride to a newer house facing the country road, a custom which had now grown to be the fashion. They lived all the days of their married life in that house. Many members of my mother's family lived nearby, for they, too, had been a part of this region for generations.

Relatives were forever dropping in, especially during the summer when those who lived at a distance came back to see the kith and kin. I could not say to them, once they had arrived, "I'm sorry—I'm writing."

"Well, stop it," they would have told me, "and come on down and be a human being with the rest of us."

Neighbors and friends also came, assuming we would be overjoyed to see them. I was not always happy at these visitations and, I fear, sometimes showed it. Word had got around that I had sold a story and often the guests were frankly curious about it. The money I had received varied in the estimates. People had read about the great bonanzas some writers received. While no one believed I had been paid a breathlessly magnificent fortune, still some of the guesses, as reported back to me, were flattering. I gave out no information as to the price I would receive or, as far as that went, as to the fact I was yet to receive it.

"What did you do with your money?" one woman asked.

"Oh," I said, with complete honesty, "I need a new watch."

Watches could be any price. The guesses continued.

But in spite of interruptions, I wrote. I would work until I was stuck, and then go downstairs and pick up an apple

from the basket sitting on the back porch. I would take it
back to my room with me and, standing in the middle of the
floor, eat it, core and all. By the time I had finished, my
thoughts had pretty well cleared up and I would sit down
and write again. I've never been able to find it in my heart
to judge Eve too harshly. I can understand very well how the
sight of an apple can give a woman ideas.

We waited for the story check. Mama was pessimistic.
"Perhaps they don't mean to pay you at all," she said. "You
should write them."

That I was reluctant to do. I toyed with the idea of going
to Kansas City, since I was so close, and having a conference
with the editor. But I discarded the idea. I think I halfway
feared my mother was right, but I preferred to live in a world
where there was yet a bit of hope rather than face the truth.

"Of course," my father said, "they'll print it in several
papers. Nobody would pay that much for a story and use it
only once."

Now and then friends and relatives would ask, curiously
and coming to the question by devious routes, just what I had
received.

"Oh, not too much," I said.

Usually they laid my answer to becoming modesty, some
of them adding a few dollars to the original estimate.

I did not tell anyone I had already written the editor, but
not for the purpose suggested by my mother. Late in the
spring I was visited by an attack of stage fright, or timidity,
or whatever *mal* is common to writers. I merely told him
I wanted the story to come out under a pseudonym. Never
ask me why, but that is the request I made. Although I had
no reply, I assumed my wishes would be observed.

I had also taken another step in the writing world. An aunt in Kansas City to whom I had confided the fact of my first sale told me about a woman in New York who, for a fee, acted as critic and agent. The aunt gave me the address of the woman, and I promptly sent her a story, together with the required reading fee. I think I halfway expected the news of a sale by return mail. What I had was a form acknowledging receipt of story and check. Beyond that, nothing more. The weeks slipped by and I almost forgot about the matter. Besides, I had something more important to occupy my mind. My first story was published in the June issue.

The magazine was late reaching me, having been sent first to Amarillo and then forwarded to me in Missouri. I shall never forget how I felt as I held it in my hand. There was no cover; my story was on page one, so it was the first thing I saw. The title jumped out at me.

GOOD MATCH

I read it through several times. This done, I took the magazine to Mama and Dad where they sat on the side porch-living room. I didn't say a word. I just handed them the magazine. Then I went back upstairs to my room, there to write the editor asking for extra copies. (I never got them.)

The next day the check came. With it was a note from the editor. He was sorry he could not see his way clear to paying me the fifteen dollars he had first promised me since, as he had already told me, the revision had not been quite up to his expectations. He was, accordingly, sending a check for ten dollars.

I went racing down the stairs to show the money to the

family. Let's face it. The manuscript of *Paradise Lost*, had it never sold, would not have been as impressive to most people as would an item in the Sunday School *Times* bought from Cousin Suzy for $2.50, cash. The world is geared like that. If something sells, it must have merit; if it doesn't, it can't be too good.

Naturally I did not show the check outside the immediate family. I did, however, regret my decision to remain anonymous. More than anything else in the world I wanted people to know this was my story. I tried to think of some dignified way to spread the word around, since a number of people in the community did subscribe to the small sheet.

I might as well have spared myself the concern. People knew. They had heard of my sale; they saw me in this story and knew it for mine. I was surprised at the relatively small amount of excitement its publication created. I think I rather hoped the Higginsville *Advance* would run a front-page account. Maybe the Kansas City *Star,* since the magazine was printed there and I was a native Missourian, would have a back page item. The only comment which came back to me was from a man who had known me most of my life.

"So that's her story," he was reported to have said. "I'm not surprised she wouldn't sign her name. It's really pretty small potatoes."

How very right he was. Small potatoes it was indeed. But he was also correct in a way which neither he nor I could possibly know at the time.

In Missouri, small potatoes are the ones we dig for the first "mess." They are the sweetest, the most flavorful. They are also the ones some people save for seed.

That was what the story proved to be be, small and unimportant as it seemed to him. The experience was rich and full of flavor for me. Moreover, it was the seed that started my writing career. I was off now, and I vowed that nothing could stop me.

Chapter Two

It had been nearly a year since I had made my first sale, a year in which I had continued writing with no success. I had almost forgotten about the story which "the woman in New York who is supposed to help writers" still had. Then one day my sister called me at school, her voice so filled with excitement I could scarcely understand her.

"Lou," she said, "there's a letter from that woman you sent your story to and I knew you'd want me to open it, so I did. She's sold it—for *seventy-five dollars*."

I sat down, very hard, on a chair next to the phone.

"Read it again," I said weakly. If her eyes weren't any steadier than her voice, she could be mistaken.

She came up with the same message on the second round, and even added a few details. The story had gone to *Capper's Farmer*, published in Topeka, Kansas. The editor hoped I'd send them more stories.

I think I said good-by, but I'm not sure. I walked out of the office, and a fellow teacher, seeing me, said, "What's happened? A rich aunt die, or something?" And I said, "No—no—not at all." Then I went to the cafeteria and got my tray of lunch (this was kraut-wieners-and-mashed-potatoes day) and settled in the nearest chair to eat.

Capper's Farmer, in Topeka. Less than two hundred miles from my home in Missouri and I hadn't known the magazine existed. The same sort of thing that had happened with my first sale. These markets had been right in my backyard, as it were.

I saw the school secretary making her way to me.

"You're wanted on the phone," she told me.

I got up and took off like a streak.

"If you're finished you'd better take your tray back," she reminded me.

I had barely tasted the menu-of-the-day, but I didn't want it anyway. I set the tray down in the proper niche and went to the phone. It was probably as I had first suspected; Blanche had misread the letter.

"Lou," my sister said, "I forgot to tell you. The woman gets a ten percent commission. Your check will be only $67.50."

"Oh, I knew that," I assured her. "She's earned it."

I realized dimly then what I have come to know very well indeed during the years I have been writing. A good agent is one of the best things that can happen to a writer.

We all planned to gather in Missouri for Christmas—my sister, her husband, and young Bobby; my brother and his wife, Sallie (we always said she never seemed like an in-law because he married her when she was so young that we helped bring her up ourselves); and our Cousin Bill who had been

junior high school and coordinator for the junior high English sections in our system. I was chairman of freshman guidance in our school, and sponsored our school paper. I worked in the classroom teachers club.

Looking back, I do not understand why I became involved in all these activities, for I am not an executive type either by wish or ability. I am not a joiner and I have scant talent for club work. The only way I can explain my multiple activities is that there was a shortage of teachers and I drew the black bean. Having once been assigned a duty, my first reaction is to get busy and do it.

I also like people and want to be with them rather than to withdraw into volunteer solitary confinement. Under these circumstances it was easy to tell myself I couldn't find time to write. That was the winter I made one of my most important discoveries about writing. You don't "find" time to write —you "make" it. And, what was even more important, time (for me, at least) doesn't come in big pieces. I learned to write while riding on busses, sitting under driers at the beauty shop, waiting for an appointment at the doctor's or dentist's office. I wrote in bed, as Mark Twain was said to have done. I discovered that in my case there was a certain procedure to be observed here. If I worked until I was too sleepy to write more, I woke myself up in the process of getting ready for bed. The right way to approach this problem was to undress first, and then, in bed with a pillow to my back, I would write until I could no longer keep my eyes open. Then I could jerk off the light and go to sleep.

I wrote and I mailed off and I got back. My sister and brother-in-law discussed the possibility of buying a new house. Bobby told the neighbors. "But we can't buy the one we're looking at," he said. "The mailbox isn't big enough to hold my aunt's returned stories."

I doubt that one has ever been made large enough to accommodate the brown envelopes which came to me that winter unless it would be the red, white and blue ones placed on street corners to receive mail deposits.

Somewhere down the line I had parted company with the critic-agent, although I do not remember exactly the reason for it. There were no hard feelings on either side. Perhaps she could find no more markets for my stories—she may even have discontinued the work altogether. At any rate, I was on my own again, yet I do not recall feeling discouraged. I suspect if one wants to write—really wants to write—he has a certain resiliency, an ability to bounce back after disappointments and rejections.

Then one day when I had gone to the post office to mail a story, I discovered a copy of *Country Home* on the newsstand there. This magazine, no longer in print, bore the same relation to Crowell Publications as *Country Gentleman* did to Curtis. I had not seen a copy before so I bought it, thinking (as every writer probably thinks on seeing a magazine unfamiliar to him) that here was a possible market. Once home, I began thumbing through it. In the letters to the editor, a farm wife had written to complain bitterly about hired men. This was an attitude I found difficult to understand.

When I was growing up on a Missouri farm, hired men were the delight of our lives. To us children, at any rate. Dad had a business in town so he rented a portion of our home place and kept hired men to help with the part he chose to farm himself. His store was close to the railroad, so all sorts of colorful characters would swing off freight trains and come

over looking for work. If a man seemed at all promising,
Dad would hire him. We children always regarded these men
with a mingling of awe and delight. Even after all these years
I could not read, unmoved, anything which would seem to
diminish their stature. I sat down to write a reply to her
complaint—what I wound up with was a journey back into
memory, recapturing some of the hired hands I had known.

The piece almost wrote itself. I was putting down something that was myself—something nobody else could have
written in exactly that same way. I did not copy any style
or material I had ever read. I had never seen a familiar essay
on hired men, but that was what this turned out to be. I
made a final copy and sent it off to the editor of *Country
Home,* together with a note of explanation as to my reasons
for writing it. I did not query first, a procedure which marked
me a rank amateur.

Country Home bought the article, paying the magnificent
sum of one hundred dollars for it. The letter advising me
of the sale came from the editor himself, Mr. Wheeler
McMillen.

"You have created an extraordinary situation in this office,"
he wrote, "by submitting a manuscript which all the members of the staff agreed in admiring. I hope the check for one
hundred dollars which you will receive in a few days will be
satisfactory recompense."

One hundred dollars a satisfactory recompense! To me, a
schoolteacher who made little more for a month of teaching.
And without anyone telling me how unique and wonderful
I was. Satisfactory recompense, indeed! While it was not the
six-and-a-half increase Dad had wished for me at the time of

my first sale, still it was more than I had yet received for a piece.

The article was frankly autobiographical, a condition which holds true for the writing of most beginners. This is all to the good. The oft-repeated injunction to "write about what you know" is sound advice. Years later I was to use the hired men article as the first chapter in my collection of Americana titled *Life Was Simpler Then*.

That was the beginning of a beautiful friendship between the *Country Home* and myself. In all, they bought six pieces —some articles, some short stories. Eventually the magazine folded. I went down with the ship, so to speak. One of my stories appeared in the final issue.

In the meanwhile I had added another magazine to my list, *Christian Herald*. I was always pleased to be able to have a story here. A great many famous writers have appeared on the pages of *Christian Herald*. Dr. Daniel Poling, who was editor at the time, was invariably kind and helpful. When, some years later, I finally met him it was as if I were seeing a good friend of long standing.

I discovered another market which was a natural for me, working with young people as I did. This was *American Girl*, and again, I found a good friend and excellent counselor in the person of Marjorie Vetter, then fiction editor.

As I wrote I was learning. No longer were my characters merely pale imitations of those I had found in the books and short stories I had read. I was writing about situations and places I could understand and know. I was learning, too, that writers must start little, building a solid foundation for their craft as they go along. Testing, step by step. Revising. Cutting out. Rewriting.

I have long maintained that the short story (which seems to have fallen into misfortune these days) is basic to all writing. There is some kinship between it and the chapters of a book. Like an article, it must have suspense, drama, characterization, and a reason for being written.

From the beginning, I wrote plotted stories. Not that I knew consciously what I was doing, but because, to me, a story, to qualify for the name, must have a plot. This meant, although at the time I was not able to put it into words, there must be a theme, a narrative question, scenes which gave a "yes" or "no" or "maybe" answer to the narrative question. And at the end, there must be some sort of conclusion, not a Lady-or-the-Tiger evasion, clever as that is, and much as it arouses our interest. Neither can it be a dwindling off, a leaving-everything-as-it-was-or-worse. This reminds me of something which happened to me when I had just come to Amarillo to teach.

My sister and I were invited to dinner at the home of some of our students. Now, we would call the family underprivileged. Then, we said they were having a hard time. The house was small, but neat and very clean. The dinner was plain, but the tablecloth was white and there were napkins. Worn, but still napkins. Before the meal, the family, together with the guests, stood around the table. Although I was a young teacher, I was older than my sister. I was "Miss Erdman"; she was "Miss Blanche."

"Miss Erdman," the mother of the house said to me, "please ask the blessing."

Never before had I been asked to do this. I did not know how one went about it, a fact I dared not admit, thinking, although I do not quite know why, that my ignorance would cast some doubts on my ability as a teacher. I shut my eyes and began groping in my memory for the words my father had used when he performed this ritual before meals. Portions from my grandfather's blessing came to me as well. I cleared my throat and began. Afterwards my sister assured me that I blessed every bit of food on the table, including each individual grain of salt.

"I thought you'd never get through," she told me. "What on earth possessed you?"

"I couldn't remember how you ended a blessing," I confessed. "I began to think I'd have to say 'Domino' and sit down."

Sometimes now when I read a short story—or, occasionally even a book—I feel that the writer experienced the same difficulty that was mine in the long gone blessing. He doesn't know how to bring the piece of writing to some logical, definite ending; instead, he dwindles off in a mumbling conclusion as ridiculous as my "Domino" would have been had I used it. (Which I didn't.)

Instinctively, I knew I did not want such weak-kneed endings to my stories. I would have a beginning, a middle, and an end and when my hoped-for readers finished, they would know they were through. And, although the word "moral" is a fighting word now, when applied to a piece of writing— especially a short story—to me, it was applicable except I called it "The idea." (Later I came to know the technical term which is "theme.") The best models are easily available —the parables of Christ which are some of the finest short stories the world has ever known. Each one has drama and suspense; each tells about real people, ones with whom the reader can identify. Each has a theme (a moral, if you prefer to phrase it that way) so crystal clear it does not have to be spelled out to the reader. In short, the parables say something. Because of this, they have lived for two thousand years.

It was my great wish that I would be able to tell something people would want to read, about people they could believe in.

I was also learning I must never say in defense of a story I had written, "But that's the way it really happened."

Nobody ever knows exactly how anything happens, not even the person to whom it happened. Least of all, him. This fact was brought out to me when I once heard several versions of an automobile accident in which a teenager and an older man were involved. A young girl who saw it blamed the older man, giving details to prove her statement. A man who was making a campaign to raise the age required for a driving license was equally sure the teenager was to blame, and quoted his version, based on facts he had himself witnessed. Both drivers had their own stories, each apparently convinced he was telling the exact and entire truth. Wasn't he there when it happened! Listening to the different accounts, I felt sure all of them were telling some of the truth, but not one of them knew exactly how the accident had happened.

Herein lies the strength and the privilege of the creative writer. He acts as interpreter, not as a journalist. He helps people to clarify, be it ever so little, their own beliefs and convictions.

I was fortunate when I was writing these stories that more markets were open to me than are now available to a beginning writer—to any writer of short stories as far as that goes. I sold enough to bring me to a state of affluence which would admit of my carrying out one of my long felt wishes—to go to the University of Southern California for a summer session.

I must confess that, once there, I spent most of my time exploring the tourist rather than the educational side of Los Angeles. I did sign up for a creative writing class, feeling a bit superior and smug as I did so. After all, I was a published writer, a state which I doubted many others in the class had attained. My complacency was short-lived. Nobody paid much attention to me, including the instructor. He read one of my stories aloud to the class and laughed at the places I had not meant to be funny. But then, we laughed at him when *he* didn't mean to be funny, so if I wanted revenge I had it. I did learn, firsthand, what palm trees looked like, and saw Hollywood Boulevard and Olvera Street and the Pacific Ocean. I counted the summer as gain and let it go at that. I came back to Amarillo and another year of teaching.

It was early in October when I came up behind a girl in study hall and saw that instead of studying as she was supposed to be doing at this time, she was reading a magazine hidden in her book. Obviously it was my duty to look into this infraction of rules. It was likewise my duty to take the magazine away from her, which I proceeded to do. Once I had it in my hand I recognized it for what it was—a confession magazine. Until now, I had seen them only on newsstands.

Under ordinary circumstances I would have told her that she could have her magazine after school. But something about the agonized protest in her face—she was obviously in the middle of a story—prompted me to withhold the promise. I was filled with righteous indignation and half-persuaded myself I should throw the magazine into the wastebasket on the spot. She was failing English, and yet she was wasting her study period on this sort of thing. I certainly should look into the story she was reading.

When my free period came I took the magazine to the teachers' lounge with me. I skimmed through the stories, surprised to find them so—well—virtuous. True, the heroines (there were no heroes in these) did wrong, but Oh how sorry they were. The recounting of their experiences was much like the skull and crossbones on the medicine bottle. "Don't do this—Beware—" they literally screamed out. I was more attracted by a full page ad announcing unbelievably large prices for stories, feeling indignation that other writers should receive such prices while my own efforts were so poorly rewarded. Not for one minute did I believe the stories represented the real experiences of the people who wrote them.

Eventually I did return the magazine to its owner, refraining from any comment. After school I went downtown to buy a copy of *Harper's* (a magazine highly approved of by English teachers). There on the rack I saw a copy of the confession magazine I had skimmed through earlier in the day. I bought it, leaving *Harper's* languishing on the stand.

Once I was home, I turned immediately to the contest rules. The story must be based on a believable situation, must have wide interest for many people, must have no more than five thousand words. Well, wasn't that the sort of thing I wrote, or tried to write, all the time? Now—to think of a plot.

As if I had conjured it up out of the air, the plot came to me that evening as I read the paper. It was an item about a young woman who had run off with her lover, leaving her husband and small child at home. Now she was asking the husband for a chance to return to him and to her child merely in the capacity of housekeeper and nurse for the child. Would he allow her to do this?

Here was a romantic situation, and real all right. Of course, I would have to find a good excuse for a woman's running away and leaving a child behind her or readers would hate her right off. I decided I would set the story in the Dust Bowl. Enough had been written about this situation so that people could understand it would make any woman willing to leave, with or without benefit of lover. I wrote the story and off it went. The weeks slipped by. Then one day the office secretary summoned me to the phone. It was my sister again.

"Lou," she said, "a letter came and I knew you'd want me to open it, so I did. You sold your confession. They will pay you a hundred dollars."

"Good—" I said, being noncommittal on the surface but overjoyed inside.

"Isn't it awful, though," Blanche wailed, "all that money and you can't tell anyone!"

Ah, that was the trouble. I couldn't tell anyone. Maybe a few in confidence—no, not even that. Confidences have a way of being passed along, strictly in confidence of course. By and by, the "confidence" is all over town. Nevermore could I walk down a study hall aisle and, with complete righteousness, take a confession magazine away from a student. Nevermore could I condemn one as being poor reading material. The secret must remain a secret except to my immediate family.

"Well, thanks for calling me," I said, for my principal was in the adjoining office, the secretary in her chair at my elbow. "I'll be home as soon as I can."

I walked out into the hall, on toward my room. Fortunately, the girl who had been the real reason for my writing the story was not in my class. I don't believe I could have faced her without being moved to apologize.

If I had thought to keep the sale a secret, I was unaware of the ways of confession markets. Once I was home that afternoon, I snatched up the letter and began reading for myself. The qualifying phrase, which my sister in her haste and delight had not bothered to read, was as devastating as the fine print in an insurance policy.

First, I must sign an affidavit the story was true, or basically so. (That was easy—hadn't I read it in the paper?) Then I must also be able to affirm that the names were fictitious. (Oh, they were, and no mistake.) Then came the clincher.

I must have the affidavit signed by some person, not a relative, who could vouch for my integrity and the fact that all the things I had said were true.

Some person, not a relative! Where could I find someone in that category to whom I would be willing to reveal my secret? I lay awake much of the night trying to think it through. It began to look as if I had been caught in the web of my own success. Better I should never have written a salable confession.

Finally I went to the last person one would think of approaching, the wife of a member of the school board. She was a writer herself and a good friend, one who had taken an interest in me and in my work. Some of the best suggestions I ever had came from her as well as some of the finest and most heartwarming and loyal expressions of friendship.

"Hazel," I said, "I've made a mistake. I sold a story—"

"Made a mistake—" she interrupted me. "Have you lost your mind!"

"——to a confession magazine," I finished. And then I told her the conditions I must meet.

"We'll go to Fancher at once," she said, when she had finished laughing. "He'll vouch for you."

"But," I protested, "he's—well—"

"If you're hesitating because he's on the school board, stop it. He's also a human being, with a sense of humor. He's going to love this—"

We wound up going together, and together telling him the nature of our errand. As Hazel had anticipated, he had a good laugh about it.

"Of course I'll sign," he assured me.

"And you won't tell?" I asked childishly.

"No," he promised. And then he added, "But I may threaten you now and then. I've always wanted something to hold over a teacher. Goes back to my extreme youth."

He signed, and I mailed the affidavit. Then I went home to wait for the check.

It came in late January and I used it to pay off bills. All sorts of bills—for Christmas presents I had charged. For doctor's bills. For accumulations that come after the first of the year. I wrote finis to the last of them, and to my bank account as well. Sometimes now, when I think I need more money for this or that, I like to remind myself of the February which followed the clearing up of those bills. I did not spend one unnecessary penny. Except, perhaps, for a ten-cent pair of shoestrings. I remember thinking it might have been possible to have sewed the broken ends of the old ones together and so saved the dime.

I went into March with the complacent assurance of one who has gone on a successful diet or saved money. Smugness

hung to me like mists around a mountain peak, but without
the becoming softness which the mist imparts. And then,
again, the call came.

(I cannot remember one time in those early years of my
writing when an important letter came on Saturday. Always
it was on a weekday; always my sister "knew" I'd want her
to open it. She was right. Success, like joy, is something to
be shared. I can crawl away with a rejection, hiding its fact
and its effect from everyone. A sale, now, is another thing
again.)

"Lou," my sister said, "you have a little bonus check. It's
forty—" Then her voice broke—something like a shriek came
from her. I thought she had been struck down from the rear,
and was on the verge of calling the police to go quick to her
rescue. "Lou—it's for *four hundred dollars.*"

I hung up the receiver, a reflex action I have never yet
been able to explain. While I sat there, the phone rang
again. I answered. "Lou," my sister said, "did you understand? *Four hundred dollars.* The operator cut us off and I
was afraid you didn't hear."

"I heard," I said thinly.

I hung up again. "Something wrong?" my principal asked.

"I have to go home," I told him. "It's almost noon, and
I'll be back for my afternoon class."

He said, "Go ahead," and asked no questions.

I called a taxi. I had to be in a state of shock to do that,
for I lived a long way from school—a full quarter's worth.
I wheeled up to my sister's house, paid the driver, and went
in.

"What's wrong?" she asked. "Are you sick?"

"Almost," I told her. "Or maybe thinking you are. Let me see that check."

"It's the prize," she said. "You've won the first prize. This is the rest of the money—in addition to what they've already paid you."

Sure enough, there it was. Four hundred dollars. *Four hundred dollars.* Made out to me. To me, who had never had a check for more than two hundred dollars in all my life, and that only a few times. To me, whose bank balance was, at the time, less than one tenth of that amount.

I held it between my fingers. I didn't say a word. I just held it. Finally I got up and started to the phone.

"You aren't going to tell anyone, are you?" my sister asked anxiously. I think she feared the windfall had unbalanced my reason.

"I have to call a taxi and go back to school," I explained hollowly.

"My heavens," she said. "I'll take you. The idea of spending fifty cents just to look at the check. I *told* you what it was."

She drove me to school. Some way I went on with my work that afternoon. You know very well what I did that evening.

I started another confession.

I embarked on an orgy of confessing. First, I confessed I was the daughter of a minister and I "went wrong" because everyone in the congregation watched me so closely, expecting me to be perfect. Of course I couldn't achieve the state of perfection they expected should be mine, so I stopped being good altogether. Next, I confessed I was a schoolteacher who couldn't live up to being watched by the community. I sold both of them, just like that. Naturally, not for more prize money, but, still for good hard cash. I was a little giddy with success.

Then, like a water faucet turning off, I lost my knack for confessing. Maybe I was unable to think of another type of person who couldn't bear watching. Maybe I got bored with writing the same thing over and over, changing only names, places, and situations. Even so, I continued to confess all over the place, to all manner of sins. Sins with which I did not have a bowing acquaintance, even in literature. I began to feel that if I stood on the busiest corner in town and shouted, "Look—I have just murdered six people—" nobody would even turn around to look at me. Not even to laugh, much less to listen.

"Your stories are too slick now," one editor wrote. "They sound professional—"

She was both right and wrong. Never downgrade the confession story. The editors who buy them have standards which must be met. They insist on stories their readers will read. A confession story must know where it is going, and not only must get there but it must also take the reader along with it. This is a good field in which to learn the craft of writing. It gives discipline and training. Besides, it is interesting to note that the confession story is one of the most highly moral types of writing in all literature. The sinner is invariably penitent and is punished for her sins, a result not always achieved in real life.

The confession editor did not give me the reason for my difficulty, although she may have sensed it. I was writing now simply because this field seemed like an easy way to make money. I had put myself into the minds and hearts of the heroines in those first confession stories. A woman who would go to pieces under the stress of prolonged and continued dust storms I could understand; Amarillo was at the edge of the so-called Dust Bowl. Country bred as I had been, I knew about preachers' daughters; some of them had been my friends. Certainly I understood the problems of a schoolteacher in a community; witness my own experience in finding someone to sign the affidavit. These people were real to me. I did not feel superior to them; I had not, as I realized was the case now, written about them with my tongue in my cheek.

Confessions were not for me. They had cast me off, rather than the other way around. This rejection, hard though it seemed at the time, was all to the good. Because I could no longer write them, I turned to something else. To stories about people and themes I could really believe in.

Years later, this fact was brought out even more clearly than I now sensed it in, of all places, a New York City beauty salon. When I came in, I found the place in a state of suppressed turmoil. Jacques, with whom I had my appointment, explained the matter to me. A famous woman writer had just left, but not before creating a great scene. "Threw a tantrum," was the way he explained it to me, his hands trembling a little as he began to set my hair. The author complained that some of the help in the lobby—it might have been an elevator boy or a bellhop or a porter, I am not sure which—had insulted her when she came in. As the incident was related to me, it seemed very minor. I question that I myself would have noticed it at all. But the author was so highly indignant that, once she got into the beauty salon, she demanded the manager of the hotel be summoned at once. When he came, she insisted the offending help be discharged.

"Surely the manager wouldn't—" I protested.

"Oh, yes—the poor boy has already lost his job—"

It seemed most unfair to me, and I said so.

"This woman, this author," Jacques continued. "She says always that in her writing she is for the underdog. It is my experience that she is for the underdog only so long as it is financially profitable for her to take this side."

He had put his finger directly on my own weakness in the writing of confessions. I was writing them only because it was financially profitable for me to do so.

Cyrano de Bergerac, that impossibly impractical romantic, put the matter very well. When approached by an emissary of the Cardinal about selling his play if he (de Bergerac) would allow certain changes, de Bergerac tells the man this is impossible.

"But when he likes a thing, he pays well," the agent says. Says Cyrano:

> Yes—but not so well as I—
> When I have made a line that sings itself
> So that I love the sound of it—I pay
> Myself a hundred times.

Money I had received for those stories, but satisfaction, no.

I did not even want to see them once they were published. Two I never saw at all. The other, the prize one, I read in a magazine purchased in the railroad station in St. Louis as I waited for my train to take me on to New York. It was a good story—I wish I had kept it. Instead, once I had read it, I left it on the seat in the waiting room, feeling as I did something of what a mother must experience in abandoning her child. I took a backward glance at it lying there, rejected, alone, and I was almost tempted to pin a note to the cover, begging the finder please to treat it with kindness and respect.

An author should not feel like this about her writing. Of course, when you do see it in print, all the weak spots show up and you will squirm at some of the obvious errors, wondering how you ever could have overlooked them in the final version. Like the proofs of your photographs, it shows up worse than you had thought it would, and you are inclined, along with the old woman in the nursery rhyme, to declare, "Laws-a-mussy me, this is none of I!"

Once the first shock is over, however, you should feel proud of your story. For its real essence is you, and no truly whole person will long indulge in self-hatred. Now that I teach creative writing I try to impress this fact on my students in the first class sessions.

"Remember," I say to them, "you are absolutely unique—"

I detail this uniqueness. As long as the world has existed there has never been anyone else exactly like any of them, with each one's identical set of experiences—of hopes and despairs, of frustrations and triumphs, of joys and sorrows. Then, just as they are beginning to feel a bit set up about their own individual glory, I cut them down to size.

"You are also absolutely universal," I tell them.

And again, this is true. No matter what happens to any one person—good or evil, happiness or pain, humiliation or success—someone somewhere will be able to say, "I know exactly how you feel. Something very like that happened to me."

Then I continue, "You, the writer, realizing these truths, must sit down with those two assets—your uniqueness and your universality—and come up with something that, but for you, would not have existed. Words that otherwise would not have been said. Characters who live because of you. Incidents that are convincing because you were able to make them so."

That is creation, and even the Lord was proud when he did it. He looked at the world, the work of His hands and He saw that, "it was good."

A writer should have that feeling about the things he has written. If there is no pride, he should either turn to something he can be proud of or quit writing altogether. I wasn't about to quit, but I was going into other fields.

The other fields were to begin at Columbia University, Teachers College. When summer came, I was off to New York. A friend of mine was going, and suggested that I join her. And, just like that, I said I would. A friend of hers had told us about a place to stay in the University neighborhood, and we wrote ahead for, and got, reservations. In early July I was in New York, ready to enroll in the summer session.

Chapter Three

The place the friend referred us to was not quite a hotel, not really a rooming house, and certainly not a dormitory, although it bore likenesses to all three. Actually it was a sort of warren, with each hutch accomodating two women. It did, however, have two important assets—it was eminently respectable, and the rent was reasonable.

Our fifth floor room faced the street—a busy one just off Broadway. The night traffic had barely tapered off when the garbage men began their rounds. We each had a narrow cot, a small dressing table. We shared a minuscule closet—no matter, our wardrobes were neither extensive nor elaborate. We also shared a study table. My cot sagged, and I suppose my friend's did, too, although I never thought to ask her. The room was dark, low-ceilinged, and five doors down from the bath where we had to wait our turn with the others who had rooms on our floor. None of these things bothered us overmuch. We would be in the room as little as possible; what we really meant to do was to see New York. I had previously made one brief trip to the city. Now I found that living here for an entire summer was different.

We joined university sight-seeing groups. We climbed to the top of everything people are accustomed to climbing in New York. We went to a night club—a very modest one, but all the same, a night club. We rode subways and the tops of Fifth Avenue busses, and the old Third Avenue El. We walked in Central Park—it was entirely safe then—and took a boat ride around Manhattan Island. We went to the brass shops on Allen Street and to a Chinese opera, and to the Village. We saw the plays on Broadway.

We roamed about seeking all the places we had read about, drinking in the atmosphere. Looking back now, I find myself smiling tolerantly at our naïveté. The things we found exciting and satisfying sound, in retrospect, like very small stuff indeed. For instance, succeeding in getting a table by the window at Child's on Fifth Avenue. The fact that we could look out on that famous thoroughfare was a thrilling experience. We tried eating at different restaurants, going down a list furnished us by the university of "foreign restaurants, inexpensive."

I remember especially a Russian place at which we were served a combination of pancakes, sour cream, powdered sugar and caviar. Maybe it was leftovers—but anyway, that's what we got. I looked at the plates uncertainly.

"How do you eat this?" I asked.

"Well," the waitress said, "you spread the caviar on the pancake and on top of that the sour cream and then the powdered sugar, and then you roll it up."

I must have looked less than enlightened, for she finished,

with some impatience in her voice, "And after that, it's up to you."

It is an anecdote I frequently relate to my classes. Anyone can give a writer advice, but eventually it is up to you, the author.

Delightful as these experiences were, they did not make the real contribution to my life except in an indirect way. Before two weeks of the summer session were finished, I knew I wanted to come back and take my Master's Degree here. Accordingly, I was sent to Dr. Ida Jewett, a most remarkable woman, who helped me plan the courses I should take. I shall forever feel gratitude to her for the interest she took in me and the good advice she gave.

Her help was more than a routine mapping out of the necessary courses. She steered me into challenging and helpful classes. She alerted me to the lectures given by the outstanding visitors who came to the campus each summer. She pushed me on, always insisting that I do more than was required of me. At all times she remained patient and helpful and, best of all, indicated that she was aware of me as a person. She made two suggestions, both of which were important to me.

First she urged me to get the degree in three summers instead of the customary four, coming for early sessions, staying on for seminars. She also felt that instead of writing a thesis I should take an extra course. She suggested that it be an advanced creative writing class taught by Dorothy Brewster.

"You have ability," Dr. Jewett told me. "I'd like to see you explore your writing potential."

When I came back the next summer, I enrolled in Miss Brewster's class.

As a prerequisite I had sent ahead a copy of one of my published stories, together with a brief summary of my writing experiences. (I neglected to mention the confessions, although I suspect Miss Brewster would have been amused rather than shocked.) Anyway, I had never confessed to an error as great as the one I am about to admit. I went into the class because Dr. Jewett had suggested I do so rather than because I expected any real help or inspiration. I am sure my thinking was colored by my one experience in this field.

I had not attended more than two sessions before I knew that here was what I had been waiting for without knowing it really existed—a good teacher of creative writing, one who was stimulating, understanding, and helpful. Miss Brewster was herself a published writer with several books of distinction to her credit. She was thoroughly at home in the great literature of the world, yet she never laid down laws as to what we should, or should not, write about. She merely took the material we gave her, and with a sure touch, laid bare its weaknesses and its strengths. We were never led to think more highly of ourselves than our work justified, yet, at the same time, no student was ever diminished in her class. There was a detached kindness about everything she said, even her most telling criticism. I suppose when one is sure of herself, she does not feel the need to cut others down to size.

My friendship with Miss Brewster has continued down the years. Later, when I myself began to teach classes in creative writing, I tried to pass along to my students some of the help and encouragement she had given me.

Just before the summer session ended, she suggested that I enter a short story, one I had written in her class, in a contest sponsored by a well-known New York literary agency and open to creative writing students in colleges and universities of the United States. First prize, fifty dollars plus the services of the agency; second place, the services of the agency only. I agreed without any hopes of winning. I could see my story lost in the flood of manuscripts I felt sure would come in.

The amazing thing was, I did win. Not first place with the added bonus of fifty dollars, but second which meant I now had a big time agency willing to market my material. Of course I immediately began bombarding them with my stories, dredging up all the old ones which had been returned to me. In common with most beginners I harbored the delusion that agents were magic medicine, feeling sure all my rejected material would now sell at once because "they knew the right editors." Also, in common with other beginners, I completely overlooked the fact that if my stories weren't good enough to sell by themselves, an agency would probably be able to do very little with them either. I suspect about all I accomplished with the flood of manuscripts was to make the people in the agency office wonder why I had ever been awarded a prize in the first place.

However, if they had doubts, they refrained from expressing them to me. The woman who evidently had been assigned to work with me sent my stories to various magazines. As each came back—and back they came, but this time to the agent instead of to me—she would forward the editor's comments which were frank and not always complimentary. Reading them, I gradually began to lose faith in my ability to write.

I was feeling discouraged about it all that day when the news came.

Sunday, December 7, 1941. Pearl Harbor Day.

Sometimes I think civilians envy soldiers when war comes.

They know exactly what role they are to play. For the people who stay at home the path is neither so simple nor so clear. They cast about them, wanting desperately to be of use, trying many things, rushing everywhere, working too hard, oftentimes doing all the wrong things. In a limited way, teachers are like soldiers. Our role was pretty well defined for us.

Already we had given our services in registering the males; already we had worked at sugar rationing. Now jobs sprang up everywhere.

There were bond drives. I spoke before service clubs. I prepared my students to talk over the radio. We sold Thrift Stamps in classrooms. We had air raid drills. We plunged into all sorts of activities, ones which seemed to have popped up overnight.

I worked in USO, too. No glamorous jobs—mine was the duty to make coffee on Saturday evenings. I worked steadily from six to ten, scarcely looking up. As fast as a container was empty I would make more. At the end of an evening my hands were red and raw. Sunday afternoons I went again, this time to check out play equipment and mail packages in an improvised post office. My headquarters were a smelly, unaired little cubicle back of a counter under a stairway. I don't know how many Ping-pong balls I issued. I lost all count of the number of packages I weighed and mailed.

I didn't think much of writing those days.

One February morning I went into the library to check on some books I needed for my class that day. The librarian, a good friend of mine, was busy placing new books on the shelves.

"Lou," she said, "have you ever thought of writing career

books for young people?" And then she added as an after-
thought, "You could—they are not very well written."

I sidestepped that one, saying I had not thought about it.

"Here," she said, "take an armful. You'll see—you can do
a lot better."

I took the four or five books she handed me and left the
room. That night, sitting up in bed, I looked them over with
a speculative eye. She was right—thcy didn't seem to be too
well written. There was a pattern to them, one which did not
greatly interest me. The next morning I took them back.

"Wasn't I right?" she asked.

"Yes," I agreed, without further comment.

"Well, when are you going to start one?"

Here was a poser. As a matter of fact, I hadn't meant to
start at all. The very thought of writing a book frightened
me half to death. A short story was difficult enough. The
books I had been examining were at least twenty times as
long as a short story, and, therefore, twenty times as hard to
write. Besides, I couldn't even sell stories any more; I would
probably suffer even worse defeat in book writing.

"I'll let you know," I said, and walked out of the library
to my class.

All day her question kept nagging at me like a gadfly
bothering a tired horse. I would brush it away, only to have
it return, bringing with it all its cousins and friends. Gradually some sort of conclusions began to emerge.

Career books were exactly what their name implied—
stories concerning the various jobs and professions. The
authors certainly must have had information about the subject with which the book dealt; they also would very likely
have some writing experience. I had done some writing; I

also knew a profession well—that of teaching. The books were about young people, written for young people. Here, too, I had an advantage for I was closely associated with this group. I felt I understood them. (One irate mother said of course I got along fine with young people—I didn't have any more sense than they had!) Finally, my *American Girl* stories, the Becky Linton series, had been very popular with the young readers. I had many fan letters testifying to this fact.

By the end of the day I was at least giving the idea some consideration. I sent word to eight or nine girls, ones I had worked closely with on school projects, suggesting they drop by my room a few moments before going home. They came, and to each I said the same thing, "I have something I'd like to talk over with you. Would you bring your lunch and eat in my room tomorrow? I'll furnish drinks and dessert."

They were accustomed to doing this when I had special assignments for them—something like a committee meeting, or plans concerning a school party, or the paper. They all agreed to come.

The next morning before classes began I went to the library.

"Velma," I said, "pick me out nine career books. For girls," I added.

She found them for me.

"I knew you'd do it," she said complacently. I let that pass.

The girls gathered in my room at noon, carrying their lunches. I had drinks and ice cream bars for them. I also had the books.

"I would like each one of you to take a book home," I said. "Read it, and then answer the questions I've written on this sheet. Next Monday, if you will, come to my room again for lunch and we'll talk them over."

They left with their books, looking important. The following Monday they were back again, suggestions in hand.

For the most part, they liked these career books. But there were adverse criticisms as well.

"No job was ever this easy," they decided. "Nobody ever went out and had things as good as this girl did."

And so it went on and on.

"There's a mystery in every one," another girl said. "I guess that's just part of it, but they get monotonous. They all sound like they are giving a lecture, too."

I filed those comments away with the others. I did not tell them what I had in mind. I thanked them and dismissed them.

That night I went home and started my book.

I didn't know the first thing about writing a book. I didn't have any idea for a plot. I hadn't even a ghost of an idea for a title. All I did know was that I was going to try to write a book about teaching, and a book was twenty times as long as a short story. In my diary for that day's entry I wrote, "I've started a book. It sounds awful. I'll probably never even finish the first chapter."

I did, though. It took me two weeks and it sounded wooden and artificial, but I had it down. Fifteen pages, as I recall. It concerned two young girls, seniors in college, who were looking for a teaching job. That situation was real enough, one that confronts every beginning teacher, and sometimes those with years of experience. With this much done, I gathered my girls in for another luncheon session.

This time, I passed around the pages of my manuscript, refraining, however, from revealing the author's identity.

Without really saying so, I meant to leave the impression I had copied someone's published book. They passed the pages from hand to hand, nibbling away on sandwiches and potato chips the while.

"They're talking silly here," one girl said. She read the portion aloud and I cringed. Silly was too mild a word.

"She wouldn't act like that," came another comment.

"Make a check mark," I told her. And, hastily, "Don't take the time to read it aloud."

"It's pretty good," they told me as they finished the last page just before the bell rang. "When can we see some more?"

"Next week," I promised rashly. "Meet in my room a week from today."

"We'll be here," they promised.

Those girls are women now, some of them married, with children of their own as old as they themselves were at the time of those lunch reading sessions. Whenever they see me, they are fond of saying, "Remember how we wrote the book?"

In essence, that is the way it went. *We* wrote the book. Each chapter, each scene, even each sentence, was checked carefully by girls of approximately the age for whom I was writing. When they objected to any part, found a portion they considered boring or unreal or foolish, I took their criticism into consideration in my revision.

Since I had written only short stories before, it was no wonder that I used the same technique in writing the book. Each chapter was actually a short story with a beginning, a middle, and an end. Each, however, was about the same people. This continuity of characters was about all that tied the chapters together.

Following the pattern of career type books I had read, I

worked in a mystery. The girls liked this part least of all. "Sounds sort of . . . well, impossible," they said.

I think we were not more than a third of the way into it when one of them looked up at me accusingly, *"You're* writing this book," she told me. "You're not copying it."

"I never said I was copying it," I reminded her.

I really hadn't. They accepted my statement. Anyway, it was more fun to be working on a real book. They insisted on making this distinction between my manuscript and published books. I was pleased.

"I'm glad you know," I assured them. "Now we can really get down to business."

We did indeed get down to business. The suggestions came faster; the girls were caught up in the joy of creation, feeling sure their own ideas would, before too many weeks, appear in print. I listened to everything they had to say, using or discarding as the case seemed to justify. I did, however, retain the mystery, changing it so that it came nearer meeting with their approval.

By now the school year was drawing to a close and I was looking forward to a summer at home. For me this meant time to write, time in which I could finish the book. I thought I saw my way clear so I wrote my agents telling them of my project. They wrote back that they were pleased. Finish it and send it to them, they told me.

Once more I packed my typewriter and headed for Missouri. This was different from the other vacations, however. With me I carried a book manuscript, completed, and needing only revision before I sent it to my agents.

My sister and her children went with me to spend a month in Missouri. Mornings, we would clear up the household chores. As soon as dinner and dishes were finished, I would go upstairs to my room and start writing. How I did hope all company would be the morning kind!

Of course, it wasn't. Friends and relatives naturally wanted to drop by and welcome us. I had to stop work and visit with them. I could not say I was writing a book, and excuse myself. That would have branded me as a "show-off" and embarrassed the family. Writing letters I might have confessed, or cleaning the attic, or even taking a nap. But writing a book—never!

In spite of interruptions, however, I did manage to do some writing almost every day, working it in when I could, setting an overall goal of so many pages a week.

It is amazing how one can use little pieces of time when a project is under way. It is as if the mind, when it starts turning, is like an engine. Less fuel is required to keep it going than to start it in the first place. It is amazing, too, how once you are engaged in a piece of writing almost everything you see or hear will give some added light. The wisdom, the information, the ideas have been there all along. We needed only to tune in on them.

I chose a title, " . . . and gladly teche, . . ." the words spoken by Chaucer's clerk. I wrote it on the cover page, feeling much pleased with myself. Perhaps nothing could illustrate better my naïveté and lack of knowledge in the writing field than the admission that I did not have a carbon. Typing was difficult at best; a carbon copy only served to make things more complicated.

Finally the manuscript was finished. I put it into a box and wrapped it in brown paper. Dad said it should be tied securely—no namby-pamby grocery store string would do the job. He found some lengths of binder twine. These he wrapped round and round the package, making every knot secure.

And so, the manuscript for my first book went off to New York tied with Missouri binder twine.

The next day a bulky package arrived, addressed to me. It contained all the short stories I had sent my agents. They had been unable to sell these stories, they reported. If I cared to try them myself on smaller magazines, it was quite all right. Attached was the list of editors, together with the names of the magazines they represented, who had seen the stories. The list contained the name of every first-string magazine in the field and a few seconds.

"And so," I wrote in my diary, "ends in defeat the experience from which I had hoped so much." A prim and stilted way to express the discouragement I felt.

But in writing you learn to bounce back quickly. You jolly well better! Before long I had a note saying my book had arrived. Even now I won't let myself think what I would have done had it been lost in the mails. No carbon!

When I went back to Amarillo in the fall of 1942, the whole school system seemed like a new place. Many teachers had gone into war work so we were shorthanded to an alarming degree. Inexperienced teachers and some who had been out of the profession for many years were coming in to fill the vacancies. The old hands were busy trying not only to carry their own load but to help the newcomers as well. Occasionally tempers flared and problems arose which seemed to defy solution. Naturally the students felt the tensions, sometimes misbehaving for no apparent reason. Teaching was not easy that year.

Of course we all felt we should do some war work also.
I continued working at the USO. *Capper's Farmer* suggested
I write an article on the work of this organization, thinking
the information would be of interest to rural mothers whose
boys were in the service. I wrote it. Marjorie Vetter, of *American Girl,* wanted some Becky Linton stories based on problems young people were facing in wartimes. I tried a few of
these, also. Outside of this, I did no writing.

The growing unrest among the students convinced me we
needed some sort of school recreation program. Accordingly,
in my role as freshman counselor, I recommended that we
buy a hundred or so pairs of roller skates and start a series of
skating parties. This was done. No sooner had the parties
begun than I realized I could manage them more effectively
if I myself learned to skate, getting out on the floor rather
than sitting on the sidelines.

I had never had a pair of roller skates on before, but I
learned now. The big boys taught me. They literally would
not let me be afraid. By and by, I was able to get around the
gym floor, most of the time on my feet. If I fell, which I did
rather frequently at first, I jolly well got up the best way I
could, just as they themselves did. Short of a broken bone,
I was expected to go right on skating again, once I was on
my feet.

The Amarillo Classroom Teachers Club, of which I was
president at the time, organized a series of dances for the
enlisted men stationed at our air base. These were given at
the high school gym. Naturally, I was supposed to attend
and do my part, along with the committees who handled
these sessions, to see that things went smoothly.

No wonder I was too busy to think much about the book

manuscript, still in the agent's hands. Occasionally, I would have a report giving the name of the publisher to whom it had been sent. Then, in due time, a notice of its rejection. The agent urged me not to be discouraged—paper was scarce and fewer and fewer books, especially first ones, were being published these days. In the meanwhile, she was continuing to show it to the various publishers.

The school year was almost ended when I had a letter from my agents. Bertha Gunterman, juvenile editor of Longmans Green, was interested in my book, but I would have to rewrite it. Would I agree to do this?

Would I agree! The question was purely academic. I sent back my affirmative answer at once, adding the information that in a couple of weeks I would be going to Missouri for the summer and mail should be addressed to me there.

To Missouri accordingly came Miss Gunterman's suggestions. They covered several single-spaced pages, and were clear and definite and made sense. Mostly I wondered why I hadn't thought of them myself. There must be literally hundreds of writers who, down the years, have also received her help and encouragement and who say, with me, "But for Bertha Gunterman, I never would have been able to write my book."

Among other changes, I would have to find a new title. *And Gladly Teach* had already been used.

Scarcely had I finished reading her detailed memo before I started the revision. This time, things were different. I was working along the lines suggested by an interested publisher. My fingers raced so fast they tangled on the keys. I was having fun. I found my title in much the same way I suspect a great many authors come across theirs, by consulting a copy of

Bartlett's, a Bible, and some of my old schoolbooks, opened
to the poetry section. Finally I came across the phrase I
wanted—"Separate Star" from Kipling's *L'Envoi*. I tied it
into the manuscript, somewhere in the middle of the book,
making it a part of Aunt Harriet's speech at teacher's meeting. I had already gone past this place in the typing of my
manuscript, so I simply labeled the page "insert" and let it
go at that.

At last the manuscript was finished. Once more Dad
brought out the binder twine, and together we wrapped it
and sent it off. This done, I waited. Then one July day the
letter came. I had sold a book. My first book. "News I
scarcely know how to write," I put in my diary. "Sold *Sepa-
ate Star* to Longmans. I still can't believe it."

My contract came a week or so later. "I waded through
every word," I reported. "Didn't understand a thing it said,
but went on and signed anyway."

I had sold a book and signed the contract. I kept telling
myself that a book is different from a short story—something
special, something extra. I wanted to celebrate so I stopped
in Kansas City on my way back to Amarillo and bought a
new dress. "A good little basic black," the saleswoman called
it. I also bought some pearls. Simulated, of course. But even
so, better than I would have bought under less auspicious
circumstances.

Once I was back in Amarillo, I showed my purchases to
my sister.

"They certainly are smart," she said. "A black dress and
pearls—"

Suddenly, I began to laugh. "Isn't that what women are

supposed to buy when they are getting ready to go to an old ladies' home!" I said.

"Well, at least you'll have more time to write there," Blanche told me.

Shortly before the birth of my sister and brother-in-law's first child I had gone to live with them. When the children came along—Bobby, the oldest and Molly Lou, my namesake —I took delight in them also. It's good to be a part of a family, to be around children. It helps to keep one in touch with reality. Now the time had come when I felt the family needed more room. So I decided to accept the invitation of a friend of mine to move in with her. She was a widow with a daughter away at school. She had just built a new house. It was a thoroughly satisfying arrangement.

It was here that the galley proofs of my book came one January day. I took a look at the squiggles and signs on the accompanying page of instructions, and realized I was lost. I called a friend of mine, a teacher, who had worked on a newspaper and knew all about proofreading. She came, and we spread the proofs on the dining room table early in the morning. At noon we ate a bit of lunch, working as we ate. My friend sugested the system we followed. I read a page first, made notations (according to her directions) and then passed it on to her. Of course she found errors I had overlooked.

At six, we stood up and came back to this world. All day we had been in another place, in the small town which was the setting of the book. We had been with the people whom the book concerned. Now, brought back to our own world, we looked at each other, blinked and said vaguely that perhaps it was time for dinner. I can't remember another day in my life that passed without my being aware of its going.

"Well," she said, "it's finished."

"I'm not so sure," I said absently. "There were one or two other ideas I've thought of that I'd like to incorporate. I think I'll write two more chapters."

That is exactly what I did. Even though it was the first of January—and the book was scheduled for March publication —I wrote two extra chapters and sent them to Miss Gunterman, who saw that they were included in the middle of the book at the place I had indicated. As I have said before, there is no way of paying enough tribute to her for all the help she gave me.

I did not have to wait for my author's copies in order to see my book. A young student whose father edited a paper in Amarillo came to me, in her hand a package. "Daddy got a review copy and I thought you might want to see it," she told me. "So here it is."

Bless her! I am sure she understood why I jerked it away from her, and probably did not even remember to say, "Thank you." She, and the others in my classes, for she passed the word along, also knew why they had written assignments that day. I was reading the book. *My* book. By the end of the day I had finished, but it required a full week to check all the papers I collected. I still think, however, there was something particularly fitting and proper about reading my book on teaching while I was engaged in an actual teaching situation.

My own copies came the following day. I opened the package, my hands shaking a little, and promptly autographed three books—one for my sister, one for my brother, and one for Mama and Dad. Next I went down to the bookstore to see if their copies had come in. Sure enough, there they were, sitting in the windows and looking (or so it seemed to me) very imposing. I graciously consented to autograph, wondering as I did, how I would have overcome my disappointment had I not been asked to do so.

A few days later Dad and Mama's reactions came in a letter Dad had written.

"Your mother and I have read your book," he said. "I don't know quite what your main purpose was—whether it was to tell a good story and entertain, or to give a picture of teaching and instruct. Whichever one you had in mind you have succeeded beautifully."

The book was widely and favorably reviewed, but none came to the point so well or stated the essentials as clearly and briefly as did Dad's evaluation. Reading the letter, I was pleased and touched. Mama would have liked what I wrote simply because I had written it, automatically making it something to cherish. But Dad's appraisal was a different thing again. He was a reader; he knew books. If he said it was a good book he knew what he was talking about. Others reading it would agree. It would do well.

As indeed it has. It is still in print. Only a few years ago it and its companion books on teaching, which I later wrote, went into paperbacks. These books have also been published in Germany. I continue to receive letters from people of all ages from all over the country, telling me how much they have enjoyed the books. Many young people say that, because of them, they want to become teachers. An added bonus which never ceases to amuse me is that one year Miss America, when asked what career she wished to follow, said, "Teaching." She gave as her reason a book she had read. Mine!

Scarcely had *Separate Star* been published when I began to receive letters from prominent people in the education world. They liked the book and felt it could serve a good purpose in alerting people not only to the problems in schools but as to the role these same schools played in the welfare of the nation. Several letters suggested that I write a companion book about rural schools, a subject recently highlighted at a White House conference on education.

I required little persuasion. When I left for Missouri that summer I already had my idea for the book.

I myself had attended a rural school, a most remarkable one, advanced in its ideas, fortunate in its teachers, unquestioned in its place in the community. Once it was even written up in the Kansas City *Star,* an honor for which we were all suitably grateful but not at all surprised. To me, a one-room country school did not mean a place of deprivation and neglect. Still, most of the letters I had received indicated this was a condition prevalent among the great majority of them now. I decided I should devote myself to some research on the subject.

I went to Warrensburg, Missouri, some forty miles away, home of the Central Missouri State College, the institution from which I had received my Bachelor's Degree. Here I got in touch with the teachers who would know most about the rural education problem. They found quantities of material —pamphlets, books, lists of sources—from which I might obtain yet more information. I went back home, loaded down with these. No sooner had I deposited them in some semblance of order than it was necessary for me to go to Pittsburgh, Pennsylvania, to a National Education meeting to which, as president of the Amarillo Classroom Teachers Club, I was being sent.

My sister and her two children by that time were home for their usual summer visit. Both she and I realized that Dad seemed far from well, although he made no complaint. She volunteered to stay until I came back, which would be about ten days. So off I went. By the time I got home, Dad had agreed to see the family doctor.

That is how the summer started, one that was to be a difficult time for all of us, which was to merge into a fall yet more strange and difficult. The doctor pronounced Dad's trouble a "heart condition," and prescribed bed rest, promising that before long he would be himself once more. Heartened by that diagnosis, Blanche and the children went back to Amarillo. I stayed on to give what aid and comfort might be indicated in looking afer my father during his illness. And, of course, to make a try at writing the book about a rural school.

I feel sure Dad realized the gravity of his illness; I think I must have suspected it as well although at the time I would not admit it, even to myself.

There is something unforgettable, almost unbearable, about the time the responsibility of parents slips to the shoulders of their children. Now, I had to assume many small duties that Dad had always taken as a matter of course. For instance, the water for the house was pumped by an electric motor. Occasionally (it had done service many years and was not too dependable now) it would stick, or stop or do something equally reprehensible. Always Dad had gone to the basement, tinkered a few minutes, and the pump worked once more. The first time it stopped this summer I had to sit down and take directions Dad gave from his bed—patiently, and oft-repeated, for I am stupid about mechanical gadgets—until I knew exactly what steps to take in order to start the water flowing again. The first time this happened, I went to the basement in mortal terror. After that I learned to accomplish my mission without shocking myself, ruining the motor, or having any other untoward accident. Mama stood at the basement steps, almost in tears. "Watch out," she would caution me. "Oh, do watch out." And then, "I declare, I'd rather pump water and carry it in a bucket than to have you down there fooling with that *thing!*"

It was under those circumstances that I wrote the first draft of *Fair Is the Morning*.

I did it for several reasons. First, I had told Miss Gunterman I would write it this summer, and once I've made a promise I'm going to make the try. Then, too, I had the feeling that if I could continue writing Dad and Mama both would feel added security. Surely, they would reason, things can't be serious, or she would not sit there typing away. Finally, the book was a sort of refuge to me. I was frightened. I felt inadequate. I felt helpless and panic-stricken. The touch of my fingers on the keys brought a degree of calmness.

During that difficult summer I began to see writing for what I consider one of its great potentials—as a kind of therapy. Not in the sense of being busy work, like a color book given a restless child. Rather, as a discipline of the spirit as well as of the mind. A self-examination. A sense of accomplishment in being able to make words give up their hidden meaning, ideas jump through hoops at your command. The ability to move into the realm of ideas and find order and sense where neither had seemed to exist. In short, a refuge where a quiet hand is laid upon the spirit. I suspect more than one writer has found this to be true.

So, each afternoon when there was no company, I wrote. It was an intensely hot summer—often the perspiration would stream from my body, run off the tips of my sticky fingers on to the keys. I kept a soft cloth nearby to dry keys and fingers. By the middle of August I had a copy of sorts finished. I sent it to Miss Gunterman, explaining that I knew the manuscript was far from right, but because of the circumstances under which I had worked, I would appreciate her checking and suggesting needed revisions.

It was soon after that that a doctor friend of ours, a specialist from Kansas City, came to see Dad. The doctor's verdict was final, concise, with no hedging. Dad would never be well again. He might linger on for months, but he would not recover.

The verdict was delivered, not to me, but to my brother and sister-in-law in Kansas City. They drove down to tell me what I think I already knew. We decided, perhaps wrongly, that it was best not to tell Mama. Knowing, she would communicate the fact to Dad. Not in words, but in her grief, for they were very close. I did telephone my sister in Amarillo, a call I made from the central office in town rather than our home phone since I did not want Mama and Dad to hear me. Blanche and I talked back and forth several times. Finally she said she would come. She had made arrangements to have the children taken care of. Vacation was almost over, and they would both be in school.

She came. She it was who decided that she would stay on and I would go back to Amarillo to teach and to keep house for Bob and Bobby. Molly Lou would be with friends during the week and then on weekends she would be at home, too.

By that time school had already started. I packed, made ready to leave. I went into Dad's room to tell him good-by. I think he knew then that we would not see each other again.

"I hate to go, Dad," I said. "And leave you sick."

"You have to go, Lulie," he told me. "It's your work. Blanche is here."

I kissed him, trying to act as if this parting was no different from any of the others. I almost succeeded. Then I was a child once more, frightened by a force I could not really understand but whose threat was clear. I wanted to say something that would be the essence of the years that were gone, a bulwark against the months ahead. What I finally said was brief, far from eloquent, but, I think, adequate.

"Dad," I said thickly, "you're the best father anybody ever had."

I turned away quickly, hoping he would not see that I was crying. No matter—I am sure there were tears in his eyes, too.

Then I was gone. Off to Amarillo and my work.

I taught and kept house and looked after the children. Bobby was in the junior high where I taught—he was even in my English class. I came out of this experience with one conviction. Every teacher should have, for two months' time, the sole care—mental, moral, physical, social—of a child the age she teaches. I learned wisdom I shall never forget. Whether he learned anything is something else again.

The call came in November. Dad died quietly, as if he were going to sleep. I went home.

After it was all over, Mama and Blanche packed and stored the furniture and other belongings they wished to keep, rented the house, and came back to Amarillo. I stayed next door with a neighbor. We all worked together to help Mama past that hard time. Just before Christmas a letter came from Miss Gunterman. She was returning my manuscript. There was much to be done to it. In fact, had she not seen a sample of what I could do in my revision of *Separate Star,* she would not even be interested in this book. But since I had done a satisfactory revision on it, perhaps I could do this, too.

The manuscript followed in a few days. I started work on it during the Christmas holidays.

As I began rereading it, I realized the first part went well enough. After that, it began to break down. I wondered why Miss Gunterman had been willing to risk revision. There were whole pages in which not one sentence made sense.

The summer in Missouri came back to me now as I sat in a rented room in Amarillo. Next door was my mother, staying with my sister. Nevermore for her—for any of us—would the Missouri farmhouse be home. There had been a complete and final breakoff in the way of life we had always known. I must have sensed this as I wrote what I was reading now. I must have known that, out of the confusion and uncertainty, a new way of life would come. No wonder I had failed to make sense.

I began revising the book, then titled *Bright Tomorrow,* working during Christmas vacation whenever I could grab a minute. I worked in January between the manifold other duties that came to me. Early in February I wrote the last page. The next day I mailed the manuscript to Miss Gunterman. At the express office with my package (no binder twine this time, but I would not let myself think of that) I found I had forgotten to bring the publisher's address with me. Never mind—I knew it anyway. I remember thinking, not without a touch of complacency, that it was pretty fine to knew your publisher's address without having to refer to your address book. I chose to consider that a good omen; I had achieved a victory of sorts.

On March 5, I received word from Miss Gunterman that my revision was quite satisfactory. I had sold my second book. For the benefit of those who think selling a book automatically solves all one's problems, makes your friend love you on sight and your hair turn naturally curly and all your teeth come in double, without benefit of cavities, I quote the entry in my diary for that day.

> Meeting after school. Home to find I had sold *Bright Tomorrow* for sure.
> That's that.
> More problems at school than I know how to meet, and in the teachers club as well.

You sell books or you fail to sell them. Either way, the problems of life continue hitting you—hard, and with what sometimes seems direct aim. And either way, you go on doing the best you can.

Letters from Miss Gunterman continued to reaffirm her approval of the book. The title, however, must be changed for there was a radio serial by the same name. We settled on Miss Gunterman's suggestion, *Fair Is the Morning,* a very happy choice I have always thought. So late did the change come, however, that I read proof under the original title.

Early in April I received a letter from the head of the English Department of West Texas State College, located at Canyon, some seventeen miles from Amarillo, asking me if

I would be interested in coming there to teach English and creative writing during the summer session. Influenced by my experience in Miss Brewster's class I felt I would enjoy being a part of a college campus, especially if I could teach creative writing. Accordingly, I asked if by any chance this assignment might become a permanent one. I was told no— they were looking for a man with a Ph.D. Which, of course, let me out on two counts—I was certainly not a man and I neither had a Ph.D. nor any intentions of working toward one. While I considered the matter, the world rocked under the impact of the news that hit it.

President Roosevelt died. We listened to the announcement and then, later, to the humble, uncertain, but curiously dedicated, utterances of the new President who had been a farm boy from my own native Missouri. It is not strange that I quite forgot about my own affairs, and had to be reminded I had not given my answer to the college at Canyon.

The year had been a difficult one, and a rest seemed indicated. I knew quite well I would not find this in a temporary summer teaching job. Even so, I could think of nothing else I really wanted to do. I decided to say yes, and wrote my letter of acceptance.

Chapter Four

Canyon, Texas, home of West Texas State College (now, University) was, at the time I went there to teach, a small town with probably not more than four thousand people, including students. It was not quite western—the presence of the school gave it an air of mellowness, a feeling for tradition. At the same time it was curiously reminiscent of a piece of the frontier set here in wide open spaces.

There were no ivy clad buildings on the campus, for the school is young, having been established in 1910. Dr. Hill, president when I came on the scene, had been a member of the original faculty. In recent years the campus has spread all over the landscape, but at that time there were only three buildings. They were yellow brick, seeming almost to have sprung up out of the sandy earth of their own volition.

My mother and I moved into a furnished duplex close to the campus, subrented to us by some teachers away for the summer. She seemed to enjoy the idea of puttering around a house while I was teaching. My freshman English classes were pretty much routine in that, like all summer classes, they differed from the regular sessions. The difference was heightened this summer by the presence of young boys just out of high school trying to crowd in as much work as was possible before, as they put it, "Uncle taps me on the shoulder." Then, too, because of the war-induced teacher shortage, men and women who had been out of the classroom for years were coming back for refresher courses in order to earn temporary certificates.

I handled my freshman English classes in much the same way I had taught in junior high. I collected papers and checked and double-checked. I insisted students correct their errors and then I checked the corrections. I held conferences. I even nagged a little. But if there were complaints about my methods, they did not get back to me. In my creative writing class I was guided by my memories of Miss Brewster. Except, of course, I did not have her assurance and skill.

I looked across my desk at that first meeting and saw nine students, all women.

"Of course, you know I can't teach you to write," I told them. "Perhaps, however, I can help you in learning to write."

They looked unimpressed. Actually they had not expected too much. Still, they were willing to take a chance. Not a bad way to pick up three hours of credit.

I really remember very little about that class. I think it went well enough. I do recall a woman, however, who gave me no end of difficulty. I later discovered she was one of a special breed, a sort of migrant would-be writer who goes about year after year enrolling in different college creative writing classes. To each new class she took with her the same pile of manuscripts. When they wore out, as they did in due process of reading and grading and evaluation, she would have them retyped (she herself could not use the typewriter) and move on to another campus. This summer she had come to me.

She told me at the first class meeting that she was writing a story about a young woman who, after "taking" one year, played the piano as no one else in the United States—and few people in Europe—could play. I myself had "taken" for several years, until my teacher told my parents as tactfully as such news can be broken that, in effect, my lessons were so much money wasted. I actually learned so little from the experience that I hesitated to question the possibility of the girl's achieving the success attributed to her.

"I am going to bring her back to Carnegie Hall for a concert at the end of the year," the woman told the class. Then she turned to me. "What do you suppose she'd play?" she asked.

Doubt came to me.

"Do you really know anything about music yourself?" I countered.

"A little. I had to be able to explain the programs I booked."

"You booked?" I repeated uncertainly.

"Yes. I booked programs for a Chautauqua years ago. Now that was an experience." Her eyes took on a dreamy look. "I remember once I stayed in a room above an office building. One night a fight broke out across the street and there was shooting. I was scared to death—I ran to the window and stood there screaming bloody murder."

"My dear woman," I said, not quite believing what I

heard, "you did that, and you are writing about music, of which you apparently know very little. Why don't you use your experiences with the Chautauqua?"

"Chautauqua!" she was shocked. "What would there be to tell about? If I did, who would want to read it?"

Chautauqua had been an American institution, going into even the smallest towns, shaping the lives and tastes and thoughts of the people. It was gone now; in another generation scarcely anyone would know it had ever existed. She had within her mind and heart a piece of Americana well worth preserving.

"I couldn't do anything as ordinary as that," she told me severely.

She not only couldn't; she wouldn't. To the end of the summer she continued writing about things of which she knew little or nothing. After the last class, she stopped by my desk to say good-by.

"I knew all along you couldn't teach me anything about writing," she told me. "Don't feel bad—you did your best."

She took her manuscripts and left. For all I know, she is still making the rounds of college campuses, carrying with her the same stories she brought to me. She was one of the group which is responsible, in part, for the uncomplimentary view some people have of creative writing classes. This is unfair. We do not blame the medical profession because of the hypochondriacs who drift from doctor to doctor, always relating symptoms, never achieving a cure. Besides—who knows. Somewhere down the line she may have gained something. If not a greater skill in writing, perhaps some inner satisfaction, some insight into herself. Or even an escape from boredom, which is in itself an achievement of no small stature.

Early in my summer I discovered my work here was less arduous than teaching junior high school had been. I was not required to supervise study halls or take my turn at duty in cafeteria or playground or hall. There were no guidance meetings, no curriculum conferences, no skating parties. Discipline problems were nonexistent. In this favorable climate I found time to revise some old stories and send them on their way to magazines which had not as yet seen them. A few stuck, which gave me encouragement.

About the middle of the summer session, Dr. Hill, the president, walked into my office. I had a moment of guilt, wondering what I had done wrong. He sat down and began to talk casually of this and that. Finally he came to the reason for his visit.

"Would you be interested in a permanent place on our faculty?" he asked.

"But you want a man with a Ph.D.," I blurted out. "I mean, that's what I was told before I came down."

He laughed, neither affirming nor denying. "Well, we want you," he told me. "Would you be willing to come?" He named a salary.

"I'll have to think about it," I said lamely.

He talked a few moments longer, and then stood up. "Let me know as soon as you decide," he said, and left the office.

The decision was not as easy to make as would appear on the surface. True, teaching here gave me more time, more freedom. But I was established in Amarillo, had many friends. Most of my activities were centered there. And the salary he had named was less than I had received in Amarillo.

My chief consideration was none of these, however, but,

rather, the matter of the Ph.D. I certainly did not want to come into a department which was unwilling to receive me.

Finally I went to one of my friends in the English department—a wise, scholarly, delightful woman. I told her about Dr. Hill's offer.

"What did you tell him?" she asked me.

"Nothing yet," I said. I hesitated, and then went on, "I think you know that when I came here I was told this would be a temporary place. You also know the reason for this. I won't give Dr. Hill a definite answer until I know how the members of the English department would feel if I came —a woman, without benefit of Ph.D., and with no intentions of working toward one."

"Oh, my goodness," she said. "Is that it! Let me tell you something. *We* are the ones who suggested he ask you."

"You——" I repeated. "You mean—the other English teachers?"

"Yes. We said that anyone who worked as hard as you did, thinking you were here on a temporary basis, was someone we wanted to keep."

I felt as if I had just received a very special blessing.

"Do think it over," she told me.

My last reason for hesitation was out of the way. I told Dr. Hill I would accept the job he offered me. Then I resigned from the Amarillo school system. This done, a friend and I went out to dinner and afterwards a movie.

The name of it was *The Valley of Decision.*

I suppose there is no real way of knowing why the memory of some childhood experiences stays with us. One comes back to me clearly across the years. Our family was driving to the

small town where we attended church. Much of our life
centered about this place. Our father's business was here.
We bought groceries and other items at the general store.
Here were the homes of grandparents and aunts and uncles
and cousins and friends. At the town's edge was the cemetery
where yet more kin lay. Just before we came to the first houses
the road topped a hill.

"If you look back at this point," Dad was saying, "you can
see one of the finest views in the whole country."

Of course we looked. Before our eyes lay a little valley, outlined by low green hills. On its surface, fields and streams and
homes and outbuildings, all indigenous to this Missouri farm
country. Self-contained. In a way, isolated. It was almost as
if the landscape was saying to us, "Look—this is a sample of
what we are like."

I had never heard the word, "microcosm," but even so, I
sensed its meaning in this view.

Only a moment, and then we dipped over the hill and the
town was ahead of us—the church and the promise of pleasure
and companionship, a thing of mind and heart and spirit.

After that I seldom came to this place in the road without
looking back. It was a habit I continued when I came home
for vacations, after I was grown and no longer living in
Missouri. I looked back the day we followed my father's
body to the church for the service before we took him to the
cemetery. I remember thinking, "Things will never be the
same again—never—never. We won't come home again as we
have always done before. But the valley will remain, and the
things it represents."

One moment, and then the view was hidden—and I looked
ahead at what must be done.

The memory came back to me now as I sat in a rented room of a rented duplex in Canyon, Texas. I looked both forward and back, remembering the region which had been a part of my growing up, something that was woven into the very fabric of my life. And, also, looking ahead to the new way of life which had begun for me with my coming to the college campus. With this evaluation of the past, this contemplation of the future, came a certain detachment, a feeling of objectivity. It was under these conditions that I started another book.

I had long held the conviction, strengthened by my father's death and burial, that if one wanted to know the true folkways of a community you went to one of its funerals. More nearly then than at times of birth or marriage you saw people as they really were. Moreover, sometimes members of the family who had long been absent came back for the services, so the three days decreed as proper to devote to the ritual brought family and friends together once more. It was almost as if time stood still, or even moved backward.

My novel as I planned it now would center on the death of an old man who had been a power in the community. At the time I knew of no books written around that theme; since then, I have found several. I had to feel my way along, with nothing much but memory to guide me. I did have a title to work toward, though. I had seen it used as the theme of a devotional and was intrigued with its implications. It was *The Years of the Locust*.

I set up my typewriter on an old library table, no two of whose legs were exactly the same height. The table faced a window which in turn faced a neighboring house, sitting very close. What I looked out on was a brick wall, and that was just about the size of it. I began writing.

There was a God-sent interlude between the closing of the summer session and the opening of the fall term. Friends were off on vacations or busy with their own activities. As yet, I had not become involved with the activities of the town to any great extent. I knew a feeling of isolation, which I found conducive to writing. I sometimes wonder whether I would ever have done the book at all had I not been vouch-safed this period of grace.

Of course I put myself into the book. Every piece of writing, and especially fiction, is in a way autobiographical. Thoreau expresses this fact most logically when he says, in *Walden,* "I should not talk about myself if there were any-body else I knew as well." But it is silly to insist a writer must experience everything he writes about. If this were true, Shakespeare would have written nothing beyond the sonnets, and not all of them; Stevenson would not have given us *Treasure Island;* Defoe would have quit before he ever started writing.

Fortunately they paid no attention to such nonsense as writing only about their own experiences. Instead, they gave us Romeo and Juliet, Long John Silver and Jim Hawkins, Robinson Crusoe and his man Friday—all as real to us, per-haps even more so, than our own closest friends.

Perhaps these writers even gained by not having lived the life they wrote about. Shakespeare, knowing a marriage that was less than happy, could dream of an ideal love; Steven-son, helpless on a bed of pain, could reach mind and heart out toward the high adventure of buried treasure and pirates and ships at sea; Defoe, constantly in the midst of political dissension, might well have thought what it would mean to live in a land untouched by the follies of mankind. They went beyond facts to fiction, which is the larger truth, the use and interpretation of facts. The reasons behind the facts. Their stories became the greatest truths; real and believable and enduring.

That is the important thing about fiction; it endures. Any math text written five years ago is to some degree obsolete. The new math has seen to that. Try a pre-space age science text on today's high school classes. Even the teaching of English is undergoing changes. Historians are constantly revising their findings about many world events, including the Civil War and the Napoleonic Wars. But *Gone With the Wind* and *War and Peace* live on. Unchanged, unrevised. True.

Already, from the experience of having written two books —both for young people, but still books—I knew people would say of different characters, "That one is so-and-so—" which again is fallacy. Nobody can set down a character exactly the way he is, even in biography. At best, you are seeing real people from the outside. Instead, a writer, even though he may begin with a suggestion of someone he knows, will make of the character something of his own—a creation touched by his own imagination, experience and philosophy. Once that character is created a most amazing thing happens —it begins to take things into its own hands. Early in my writing career, I wrote in my diary, "I am having a difficult time with my heroine. She refuses to marry the man I have picked out for her."

That is not to say a writer can turn loose of the character he has created, leaving it absolutely to its own devices. But trying to push a character into a preconceived form is not only difficult, it is disastrous.

I wasn't writing to a formula, but neither was I writing as if I were playing a Ouija board. Well and good I knew that much of what I wrote would probably find its way into the wastebasket, that every portion retained would be carefully and endlessly revised.

At the time, it did not occur to me that I was taking a difficult approach, one which I afterwards discovered almost doomed my book before it ever had a real chance. I chose to tell the story from five different points of view and wrote in flashbacks. In a way, I was like the bumblebee. By all the laws of physics and nature and science and dynamics, he isn't supposed to fly. He's built completely wrong for it. But a bumblebee has never studied physics or any of those subjects which forbid his flight, so he keeps right on flying.

Nobody had told me this was the wrong way to write a novel, so I kept on setting things down.

I discovered, however, that with a book of this length I should work out some system of filing my notes. I did this by taking the Manila envelopes in which my stories had been returned (of these I had no lack) and putting on each the name of one of the five characters. When an idea came to me I wrote it down and filed it in the envelope bearing the name of the character I felt would be the one most likely to say, do, or think that particular thing. It was amazing how little shifting was necessary once I got to the typewriter. All the time I was testing the characters, the situations, to be sure they were valid and believable.

Gradually I was finding myself going beyond sympathy for my characters, a state of mind promising little more than to "feel sorry for," implying a remoteness and a condescension. I had come to empathy, which mentally puts oneself in another's mind and heart. We have known this feeling from the beginning of our own reading experience. We did not feel sorry for the Ugly Duckling; we *were* that unloved, unwanted, unfortunate little creature. When he came into the harvest of love and beauty and appreciation, it was our triumph as well as his. We attained this state because the author himself did not stop with feeling sorry for his hero; he *was* his hero.

I was growing to know these people about whom I wrote. I do not mean in the sense that I had talked with them, or gone to parties with them, or that sort of thing at all. I had to know them in my heart. To do this I had to study real people wherever I met them. Listen to them. Think about them.

Once you've begun to do this you'll discover that at the core of each life, no matter how fortunate the person may seem on the surface, there are hurts and frustrations and despairs, problems that defy solution, hopes that never can be fulfilled, hearts that beg for understanding. And, having made this discovery, you will want to incorporate it into your writing. Such writing, however, implies complete involvement and does not come easily.

"I wept when I read your story," a woman once told Dickens.

"Madam," Dickens retorted, "that is not to be wondered at. I wept when I wrote it."

Certainly it is not necessary for an author to drip tears all over the pages. A writer should avoid oversentimentality and purple prose as he would avoid the plague. Restraint is a quality as becoming to writing as it is to an individual. But you do need that feeling of empathy, which is the language of the heart. I was feeling it for my characters. I knew what Allison Kenzie's reaction would be to the small town and limited outlook of those around her. I could understand why she would want to get away. I could go with her to Kansas City, which I knew, and to New York where I had spent three summers in school. I knew how she felt about the depressing, impossible room where she first stayed; it had been mine. Because the grimy bathtub resisted all assaults with brush and cleanser, she must line it with newspapers before taking a bath. I myself had done this. Her second apartment—the one overlooking Riverside Drive and the Hudson—that I also knew. I had felt, as she did, a sense of release when I moved in.

I could not, except in my imagination, know about the literary agent's office where she went to work. I had never been inside one. I had read about them in books, however, and decided I could manage with my academic knowledge. Literary cocktail parties were also foreign to my experience, but I reasoned they would probably be rather like others not given expressly for authors. Hollywood I had seen from a respectful distance. I think perhaps this was all to the good. I was not bound too much by facts, and so could let my imagination take over.

A wonderful gift—imagination. Well illustrated, I think, by a story some friends of mine like to tell about a small boy in their neighborhood who looked with favor on their five-year-old daughter.

One day the boy appeared at the door holding two small sticks. "I have just killed two rabbits," he said, holding out the sticks. "I want you to take them and make Her—" he nodded toward his small beloved who stood, overcome with shyness and delight, "a fur coat."

The little girl's father took the sticks and said gravely, "Thank you. They will make a lovely coat."

And he was right.

A real rabbit skin, made into a real coat would, in time, have pulled loose at the seams or worn thin. Or worse still, someone would have sniffed disdainfully and said, "Rabbit skin—Huh!"

As it is, the gift has lived on in imagination—beautiful and untouched by time. Like Camelot, which may have been a bit grubby in actual history, with garbage lying in the street. Or Helen of Troy, who could, for all we know, have had dandruff or used the wrong toothpaste.

I had created my characters in this book, and I could make them, within reason, what I believed them to be.

Seldom had two people been less alike than Allison Kenzie and her sort-of cousin, Elaine. Where Allison rebelled and left, Elaine stayed behind, a victim not so much of the climate in which she lived as of her own weaknesses and indecision. But like Allison, she was also the sum of all that had happened to her.

Miss Laura Meeks was another thing again. Small towns are often thoughtlessly cruel to the unmarried women in their midst. When *The Years of the Locust* was first published, and many times since, I have had someone assure me that she knew exactly who Miss Laura was in real life. I can answer with equal certainty that she was no one person, but rather a combination of a number of women I had known, some of them married and mothers, all of them having one quality in common. They were trapped in their own bitterness. For them I could feel a kind of pity, a sympathy. And a wonder as to why they should be as they were.

I did not have to fumble for the setting of my story or the way of life it told about. I was looking back on life as it had been in this Missouri community where I grew up.

I wrote, I discarded, I rewrote. Some of the portions which seemed best as I wrote them eventually found their way into the wastebasket. My experience with the revision of my first short story had taught me that no matter how good a character, a scene, a situation, or even a paragraph—how poetic or moving a description or a bit of dialogue—if it didn't belong in the story, off with its head. It is still difficult for me to convince myself and my students that anything, no matter how wonderful it seems, should be left out unless it contributes something to the story.

The plan was coming clearer. I wrote in my diary, "As I see the book now, it will have three parts, each representing one day." I worked with a feeling of urgency, knowing that before long school would begin and I would be back in the classroom.

Certainly this time between semesters was not without its own special events which took me away from my writing. Japan surrendered, and we celebrated in our own way, without thinking in the least of what it would meant to our own school later on. The fall term opened, and I was off on another year of teaching, with classes both on the campus and at the evening school.

Early in the fall a pleasant interlude came. *Fair Is the Morning,* the second book in the teaching group, was released. I went to Amarillo for an autograph party. Reviews

came in, uniformly good. Mrs. Roosevelt devoted her entire
"This Is My Day" column to the book, since at that time
the rural school situation was one of her interests.

I received many letters about the new book. The editor
of the NEA Journal wrote to ask if I would do an article
for the Journal. I did. A writer's magazine also asked for
an article. I did that, too. *American Girl* wanted another
Becky Linton story. I had one on hand; I revised it and sent
it off. And, made bold by my success, I sent a story to
Woman's Day, one the agents had returned as nonsalable.
It sold also. For these and other reasons, the novel was
pushed aside.

As yet I had told no one I was writing another book. I am
superstitious about this matter. I think it is bad luck to
talk about a piece of work you are doing until much of it is
already written. Under no circumstances will I allow a student to tell me what he is planning to do. "Write it out,"
I insist, "and then let me see what you have done. Talking
about it ahead of time takes out all the fizz, like uncorking
a bottle of champagne and leaving it standing open. Write—
then talk."

The writing, however, was so buried in other activities
that it seemed almost incidental. I wrote in my diary, "Trying to work on the *Locust.* Each time I try, I wonder why
I do." In the days that followed I recorded a variety of activities, none of them writing. Some talks. Out-of-town company. A four-way conversation, via phone, among my mother,
my sister, my brother in Missouri and myself, arranging to sell
the home place. And, for me, a week in the hospital, laid low
by mine ancient enemy, bronchitis.

Naturally, papers and other school duties had piled up in

my absence. It was almost a month before I wrote in my diary, "Had another fling at the *Locust*."

From that time on, I seem to have worked with more continuity and purpose. Of course, my writing was interrupted by teaching and other manifold activities. An entry says, "I wrote steadily today (Sunday). About noon, in drives a friend (I name her) with two children and one husband, and I threw together a dinner of sorts."

As soon as they left, I went back to writing.

Slowly the book was taking shape.

The friend who had helped me on my two teaching books came to a party in Canyon. Since it was Saturday night and she would not be teaching the next day, I suggested she spend the night with me. She agreed, and once we were home we began catching up on gossip.

"Are you writing now?" she asked.

"It's a moot question," I told her.

"You're writing," she said. "I can tell by that cagey air you put on. Let me see it."

I brought her the manuscript and then went to the kitchen, saying I would make coffee. When I came back with the mugs and the necessary trappings, she looked up at me and even before she spoke, I knew what the verdict would be.

"Lou," she said, "you have something here. It's good. It's different, and yet it has a universal quality."

"You think so?" I asked hollowly.

"I know so," she told me. "If I were you, however, I'd have a professional typist do the final copy. Typing is a routine job. It's better for a writer to spend the time on further writing. Or, in resting up from having written."

I agreed, but for a reason I did not give her. I had read

in a writer's magazine that Dodd, Mead and *Redbook* magazine were sponsoring a joint novel contest. The prize was $10,000. I had decided I would ask my agents to enter my novel. I could understand that a well-typed copy would be to my advantage.

I had a goal now, a deadline. I wrote as consistently as I could, working around a schedule of teaching and various other activities which are a part of life on a college campus. Of course, I maintained my contacts with friends and family in Amarillo. Early in the spring, the duplex we rented was sold, which meant we must find another place to live.

On the surface, it did not sound too difficult. But already veterans were coming back to enter school on the G.I. Bill, and we knew many more would be arriving for the fall session. Families were moving into town also, anticipating the return of sons or husbands. There was simply not an available house, or at least, not one I could locate.

Just when I was ready to give up hopes, thinking perhaps I would have to pitch a tent or dig a cave, I was told I might rent one of the Pueblos. I knew vaguely about them, a row of faculty houses just at the edge of the campus. Although not luxurious, they were convenient and the rent was unbelievably reasonable. Without even bothering to go by and take a look, I gratefully accepted the offer.

The matter of housing taken care of, I turned back to the book. I found a typist, gave him the first chapters, revised the ones which followed, feeding him sections as soon as they were ready. I wrote the dedication, the most obvious one I could have hit upon: "To my family, for reasons they know well." Finally the typing was finished, and I mailed the package to my agents in New York. I sent a separate letter asking that the manuscript be entered in the Dodd, Mead-*Redbook* contest, and relaying the information that I was going to Missouri to spend the rest of the summer. Mail would reach me there.

Then I went about the business of closing a school semester. We packed our things and stored them at my sister's until such time as I would be able to move them into the Pueblo we had been promised. This done, Mama and I set out for Missouri.

There was a certain poignancy about the situation. The aunt in whose home we were staying lived in the house where my grandparents, Mama's mother and father, had lived. All sorts of childhood memories clustered around the place. Then, too, when we sat in the yard or on the front porch—Missourians are inveterate yard and porch sitters— we could look out on a familiar landscape, one that was subtly different now. Nothing had moved—the house we had called home, the building which had housed Dad's store, the church. But now, none of them were as they once had been. It was like looking through the wrong end of a telescope, with everything out of focus. Or, like shaking a kaleidoscope. All the same pieces are still there—but now they have fallen into a different pattern.

"A letter for you," my uncle said one morning when he came in with the mail.

One glance told me it was from the agency, so I excused myself and went upstairs to read it. After all, I had told no one about my wish to enter a contest, so why break the news now. Once in my room, I opened the letter.

I read it and then went back to read it again, not quite believing what I had seen the first time. The agency, or so the letter said, had no intentions of following my suggestion. The woman with whom I had been working, and who had written the letter, said she herself had not found time to read the manuscript but one of her assistants, a young man, had done so and reported that it had absolutely no promise and should be completely rewritten before it was shown to any publisher.

I sat there holding the letter, trying to face up to its contents. She had not even bothered to read the manuscript herself; instead, she had blithely passed on someone else's verdict. She had sold two books for me, and yet she did not give her personal attention to this one, accepting, instead, another reader's pronouncement that I rewrite it.

Rewrite indeed! I was not about to rewrite that book until at least one publisher had seen it. A daring thought came to me. Until a certain publisher had seen it—namely, the ones who were sponsoring the contest. The Dodd, Mead-*Redbook* people.

I did not know at that time how one went about getting a manuscript away from an agent. I had some sort of notion that the relationship might be an until-death-do-us-part pact, one from which I could not withdraw without using devious methods. Still possessed of my anger, I wrote to the agent. I told her to send the manuscript back to me and I would see what I could do. Of course what I meant to do was to enter it myself, but I hoped she would think that I would rewrite as her assistant had suggested. The letter finished, I walked down to the post office to mail it myself in time to catch the eastbound train.

Some ten days later, my uncle came in with a box—no mistaking its contents. So they had sent the manuscript back without question.

"It's wet," he said. "Fell in the water when they threw it off the train." (Blackburn was that kind of town. The fast train threw the mail off, not stopping or minding much where it lit.)

I tore it open. Sure enough, the first few pages were damp. I went upstairs and retyped them. This done, I came down with the box under my arm.

"I'm going to town," I said.

I headed for the general store.

"I need a box," I said. "I want to mail something."

The owner, who had known me all my life, took a men's underwear box out from under the counter. "Here's a good stout one," he told me.

I put the pages in the box. They fitted exactly. Good omen, I chose to believe.

"Here," he said, "I'll wrap it for you."

He did, and I walked the short distance between the store and the post office.

"I want to mail a manuscript," I told the postmistress. She, too, had known me since the day I was born. Not for anything, however, would I have told her I was entering it in a contest.

She placed the box on the scales.

"Loula Grace, honey," she said, "I think I should tell you that you can send it cheaper by express."

I considered the matter. Time was growing short; the final date for closing the contest was close at hand. I thought the mails would be a little faster than express.

"I think I'd rather mail it," I told her.

"Fine," she said, evidently pleased I had made that choice. "It will be a dollar and seventy-seven cents."

I paid her, and then she turned back to the mail which had just come in. "You have a letter here," she said, handing it to me.

I went out of the small building and walked down those streets I knew so well, reading my letter as I went. It was from my sister. She had talked with the moving van company; they had said they could pick up the furniture sometime within the next two weeks. It might be well for me to go out to the home place and tell the people living in the house to expect the van and allow the furniture to be taken away.

A friend drove us out that afternoon. I went upstairs where the furniture and other belongings were stored. They had a sad dejected look, the mute, uncomprehending hurt of aged parents, neglected by their children. "Why have you done this to us?" they seemed to ask. "We served you well for many years. And your grandparents before you, and, in some instances, a generation before them."

I reached out to touch a chair. "It won't be long," I whispered. "Be patient."

Then I went downstairs and delivered the necessary instructions.

This done, we left. When we came to the place where I had so often looked back, I thought I could not bear to do so this time. Something was forever ended. Once the furniture left the place. . . .

And then a thought came to me. I don't know whether it was my own or one I had read somewhere: "Those who cannot look back are not able to look forward."

Suddenly it all came into focus—the pull it had for me, the meaning. Frightened people dare not look back. Mixed-up people rarely cease turning backwards. But it is good to stop occasionally and give thought to what has gone before. To take an inward glance, with honesty and compassion and understanding—perhaps that is therapy for anyone, writer or not. I turned my head just in time to see the lovely valley.

Always before I had accepted it as a unit but now the individual components began to stand out in my mind. Sorrow as well as happiness had visited these homes; failure and success, pettiness and generosity. The people had, upon occasion, been compassionate and concerned about the welfare of others; again, these same people had been small-souled and bitter. The valley had known scorching droughts, times when both people and vegetation withered away. Floods had visited it, destroying not only the crops planted there but the hopes of the people as well.

But there had been more good years than bad ones, and for the most part people had risen above their misfortunes and their weaknesses. I was right in thinking this valley represented a microcosm of life. And when you stood back far enough, as I was doing now, to take the long view, you could see it was good.

That's my book, I thought. I was looking back as I wrote it, taking the long view. Had I stayed in Missouri, or even if I had continued to come home for vacations to find everything the way it had always been, I could not have written as I did. Fielding says that setting down a thing in writing makes it a lasting memory. I had taken the backward look my father had recommended and had written about the way of life I had known. If nothing else ever came of this book I would still have my lasting memory.

We drove on. The valley dropped out of sight and soon we were in town once more.

The next day my mother and I went back to Texas.

Chapter Five

The Pueblos were ten small stucco cottages just off the campus. Pale yellow in color, Spanish in style as their name would indicate, they had been built originally to house students, but by now had come to be occupied primarily by faculty families. Numbers one through five were on a curving street so that nobody without benefit of compass could have any notion of the direction he faced; six through ten sat straight with the world, looking due south. There were almost no front yards to speak of, but the backyards seemed to have no end. Perhaps a mile away was the beginning of the Palo Duro Canyon. Along its rim McKenzie and others had fought battles with the Indians, helping to assure this region for the white man and his heirs and assignees forever.

In one of the tributaries of this same canyon, Coronado and his men had camped with the Tejas Indians in 1541, pausing on their way to search for the Seven Cities of Gold. Here they celebrated a Thanksgiving service some eighty years before the one at Plymouth Rock. The canyon was also the site of an ancient buried Indian village.

The Pueblos themselves formed a village of sorts, one that had considerable meaning for our school. It is safe to say that a number of excellent teachers stayed on our campus because during those first months they were assured of a place to live at a very reasonable rent. And something else not to be treated lightly—a community of interest with other young college couples who were also living on a low budget.

The houses were not inhabited solely by young professors and their families, however. The dean of the college and his wife and small daughter lived in one briefly; a few professors with teen-age children stayed in them occasionally. And my mother and I moved into Pueblo Number Three and lived there for ten years.

It is difficult to realize how fast those years went, how much was crowded into them. The houses are run-down now and shortly to be demolished in order to make way for new buildings on the burgeoning campus. Occasionally I drive by them and my heart never fails to do a faint remembering flip, especially when I pass the one in which I lived. William Allen White once said that heaven was a place where all the couples were young and all the children were babies. If his definition holds true, we were living right in the middle of heaven.

Each Pueblo had three rooms of equal size (small) on one side, all opening into a wide hall. On the other side of the hall were the kitchen and bath. The front and back doors were in direct line with each other. The houses were not without charm, however. The ceilings were beamed in dark rich oak. The floors were also oak, with the wide boards now held in high esteem by decorators.

Our furniture arrived from Missouri in due time and we were able to fit it into the rooms with greater ease than I had thought would be possible. We unpacked the dishes and silver and the old familiar cooking things and stored them in shelves and cupboards. We hung pictures. When we were finished, the effect was highly satisfying. It was almost as if the house and the furniture were saying, "Thank you for bringing us together. Obviously we were made for each other."

The neighbors dropped in—young women, themselves new to the campus. Most of them had children. My mother sat in a chair in the backyard under an elm tree, and the children gathered around her, calling her "Danna," the name her own grandchildren had given her. And she who had never known any life save that which was centered in Missouri, as had been the lives of her parents and grandparents before her, fitted in much in the same way her furniture did. It seemed right and natural to see her there, a white-haired woman, part of a college community.

That was the year the veterans came pouring back to campuses all over the country, and our school, like the others, was crowded. Actually, we had to delay opening the fall semester in order to find housing for them. Married couples were provided quarters in a colony of boxcarlike houses. Nothing fancy, but a place to stay at nominal rent. The dormitories were bursting at the seams, and classes were running over. At the time, we were mostly concerned with the vastly increased number of them. What we did not foresee was that with the coming of the veterans the whole wide world

was making its way to our campus. They were recently returned from Europe and the Far East and the utmost corners
of the earth. Where last year our entering freshmen might
have been able to discuss the junior prom as their most interesting experience, now the students could, and did, talk
about the Battle of the Bulge, conditions in wartime Germany, and the appearance of Hiroshima after the bomb was
dropped.

Not only did these veterans represent a divergent range
of interests and experiences, they presented, as well, wide
variance in scholastic ability. Some of them had been out of
school for a number of years, and were drawn back by the
advantages of the G.I. Bill. Others had interrupted their
college courses to go into service.

We also had the usual crop of young people graduated
from high school the past spring with no military experience
at all. Everyone realized this mixture would make teaching
more difficult than usual. As a partial step toward meeting
the problem, placement tests were administered to all entering freshmen. The results of these tests were used to some
degree in class grouping. Especially was this practice followed
in the English department. At the end of the first week it was
necessary to do some shuffling. In the process, the top group
came to me. I walked into my classroom, and this is what I
saw:

Thirty-two students, twenty-eight of whom were boys, although "boys" was scarcely the word to apply to them. Later
I was to discover that of the twenty-eight, twenty-five were
veterans. I had one or two ex-majors, a sprinkle of former
lieutenants, a few who had worn the sergeants' stripes, and,

of course, a bunch of just ordinary garden variety ex-service-men. So far as I know, no generals.

They made little attempt to hide their disapproval of this new class arrangement. Word had got around that I had recently been teaching junior high school. They were not only willing but capable of learning. Had not their placement scores proved this? Now they had been shifted to a teacher who would probably set them to diagramming and writing themes on "My Day At The Fair."

I wanted to tell them I was no happier with the change than they themselves were. My other classes were off and going fine, and I did not look kindly upon having to start all over with a new group. Besides, I was scared to death of them. I played the first session safe by asking each one to write a brief sketch about himself—his background, his interests, his hobbies, if any. I saw some tongues in cheeks, but the assignment kept them quiet most of the hour. I made the next day's assignment, and then the bell rang.

"Have a hard morning?" my mother asked when I went home for lunch. And I said, "Oh, no," and didn't fool her a bit.

I had a series of hard mornings. One thing came to my rescue, however—a determination not to let them take me in. After all, *I* was the teacher of that class and they better believe it.

They believed slowly.

At the beginning of the second week, I walked into the class to hear a low whistle from the back of the room. I looked up and, for a wonder, caught the guilty one; for a greater wonder, I remembered his name. I am not good at names.

"Oh, Mr. Jones," I said (only I didn't call him Jones, for that was not his name), "Thank you. You don't know what that did for me. It's been rather a long time since a young man whistled at me."

Reluctant laughter broke out in the room. I had scored. Not enough to count a victory, but enough to give me an edge.

I question that any leading lady ever worked as hard in preparation for opening night as I did for each session of that class. I knew my subject matter thoroughly; I worked endlessly thinking of challenging assignments. I never completely turned my back on the class.

And finally, either tired of dissent or willing to admit I could teach them something, they ceased to give me any difficulty and became one of my most satisfying and rewarding classes.

Not only had the veterans touched far shores, many of our other students came from distant states. One day a young boy who, I felt sure, had never been west of his native Brooklyn, needed a book which was checked out at the college library. Since I had a copy at home, I sent him to the Pueblo with a note to my mother saying he might borrow the book.

Later when I came home, he was sitting at the kitchen table, talking between mouthfuls of homemade bread, the book entirely forgotten for the time. The word got around, and after that I often came in to find the same scene—a boy, not always from far away, but sometimes one from some small town close at hand, sitting in the kitchen eating slice after slice of hot bread while Mama beamed on him.

My problems were by no means over, however. I had been

hired to teach not only Freshman English but Creative Writing as well.

Creative writing classes are in strong disfavor now in some circles, but it is neither practical nor possible to dismiss them with a blanket indictment. Too many excellent ones are taught on college and university campuses throughout the country; too many gifted teachers, some of them respected writers in their own right, are guiding students who are themselves writing exciting and worthwhile material. I myself have taught a creative writing class since I first went to Canyon. Some fine work has come out of those classes of mine. A gratifying number of books, articles, and short stories have been published, work either done while the students were in the class or after they had ceased to be members.

Not for one moment have I ever thought that I taught these people to write. No one can be taught unless he has the wish and the ability and the willingness to do the work which writing requires. I have felt, rather, that my classes surrounded the would-be writers with a climate of writing, and with others who were interested in what they were doing. The class members offered criticism and encouragement when this was indicated. I believe such a class can, in common with classes in all the other subjects, vary from excellence to mediocrity, or worse.

My campus class in creative writing went well enough. It was the night class which presented difficulties.

At this time our evening classes met in Amarillo. The enrollment was varied. College students wanting a course which for one reason or another they were unable to work into their daytime program. Townspeople, finding this an interesting and convenient way to return to school. Teachers from the surrounding towns who needed to pick up credits. Some people drove in for a hundred miles or more for these night classes. And since we were not too far—as distance is counted in this wide region—from the border of both New Mexico and Oklahoma, we had occasional students from these states as well. Our class enrollments represented all ages, interests, and, of course, degrees of talent. Especially was this true of my creative writing classes.

There were those of course who came from sheer curiosity, thinking it a good way to kill an evening, much as they would have gone to a movie or got up a bridge game. Others seemed confident they had only to attend a semester of creative writing and then go out to write the Great American Novel, winning fame and glory (and much cash) in the process. All in eighteen weeks. But there were some who came with something in their hearts they wished to say and a great wish for help in the saying thereof. It was this group I wanted to help. I knew I would not be able to do all they hoped for, all I would like to do. I comforted myself with the Chinese proverb, "Teachers open the door; you enter it by yourself."

In the only two writing classes I had known, the teacher read aloud from the stories handed in by the students. Even with Miss Brewster's cool, impersonal detachment, the process, to me, was one of exquisite torture. I would watch the author of the story which was being read and suffer with him. It was like seeing a bug impaled on a pin; it was exposing one's psyche, naked and helpless, for all the world to see. Yet I knew of no other way to approach the problem. So I assigned stories to be handed in at a certain date, planning to do as I had been done by— read them aloud myself and make the comments I felt were both justified and necessary.

But fate intervened. The night the stories were handed in, I came to class with a case of laryngitis. I regarded the group, wondering how best to handle the situation.

"No need to tell you I have a bum throat," I croaked. "Who will volunteer to read his story to the group?"

There was a moment of silence. Then a young woman of considerable talent and few inhibitions volunteered.

"Do you mind coming to the front of the room?" I suggested.

"You mean—stand up."

Like a recitation. Like a child saying a speech.

"Oh, no—" —and again inspiration came to me. "Here—you take my chair."

A moment of uncertainty and then she came forward. I slipped back into the chair she had vacated. The psychological effect was immediate—I was, in a manner of speaking, no longer the teacher but one of the students. A part of the audience, as they were.

She sat down. She cleared her throat. She began to read.

The story was average. Not bad; not world shaking. Like most young writers, she had written about herself without using her own name. It had little or no plot and was, although she would have been the first to deny it, a sort of unconscious plagiarism in that she had taken from the books and stories she had liked such episodes as had moved her. These she had changed, giving new names and new settings to characters and locations. Almost invariably, young writers start off in this way. Like a child learning to talk, they use the words they have heard. As I recall, it was supposed to have deep Social Significance—a combination of Faulkner, Eudora Welty, and John Steinbeck. Still, she had put her own stamp on what she was writing, and she had got something finished. I listened with interest, making notes as I did so, thinking that reading her own story at least gave her something to do with her hands besides biting her nails.

Once she had finished she started back to her seat.

"Just a moment," I said, "why don't you stay there so the others can make criticisms and suggestions?"

She accepted the dictum as a doubtful blessing but agreed.

"Now," I turned to the class, "what do you have to tell her about the story?"

I don't know what quirk there is in human nature which makes people assume that criticism must be adverse. The members of the class began at once to tear the story apart. Their comments were candid, minute, and almost invariably uncomplimentary. The author wilted visibly. I felt dismay; the very thing I had hoped to avoid was taking place. Under the capable hands of a good teacher, such treatment might have value. Here, it had taken on the dignity of a wrecking crew.

I got up, made my way to the front of the room and nodded to the author, who by now was completely demoralized. She slipped back to her seat.

"Just a moment," I said to the class. "I should have explained to you what I believe to be the true nature of criticism. In its best sense, it is creative. Here. . . ."

I outlined for them a plan which, in essence, I have used for my classes until this day. First, it is necessary to find something good about the offering, if nothing more than to look upon it as a piece of creation, a thing that, but for the author, would never have existed. Second, the critic should say, "*In my opinion*, such and such things are wrong"; and finally, "In my opinion, they could be corrected in the following ways."

It is amazing how that last item sets critics back on their haunches. The class was silent, considering these guidelines which I had put before them. Finally one of the students spoke up—an older, more mature man who had made no previous contributions to the class. His comments were brief but well taken. Soon other members of the class were joining in, their criticism more thoughtful now, more logical. The young author, so recently torn to pieces, was being put back together in a manner of speaking.

At the time I had thought only to rescue the author. What I could not realize was that the greater help came to those who gave, rather than to those who received, the criticism. For in thinking of ways to improve their criticism, the critics were helping themselves see their own weaknesses and, seeing them, strive for improvement. It is easy for criticism to degenerate into mere nit-picking; in its best sense, it is an art. This of course I did not realize at the time. I knew only the class was going better—that it was more nearly achieving the goal I could wish for it. I felt I was making progress.

Only my mother expressed concern.

"Loula Grace," she said, "if you teach everybody to write, who is going to buy your things?"

Indeed, my students have, down the years, had material published which I, or any other writer, might have been proud to claim. But always I have felt only pride and satisfaction in their accomplishments, as I am sure any teacher does when she sees her students succeeding.

It is understandable that with the business of getting settled in a house, of starting classes unfamiliar to me, I should have scant time to think about a novel I had entered in a contest some four months ago. If the thought came to me at all, it was to realize there must be literally thousands of writers from all over the country who had sent in manuscripts, hoping, as I hoped, they would win. It was like reaching into a grab bag blindfold. It was like buying a ticket in the Irish Sweepstakes. Had I won, I would have already been notified. I remembered that I had not enclosed the $1.77 for return postage, which was careless of me. Perhaps I should send it now if I wanted the manuscript, which I most certainly did.

Then came the letter. Friday it was, November 8. From Dodd, Mead, bearing the signature of Mr. Edward Dodd. The sense of it was that they were considering my manuscript but wanted to know a little more about me before making the final decision. They would like a biographical sketch, and also, to know whether I was planning a career as a writer, and did I have any more novels in mind, and were any of the characters drawn from real life.

I recorded the event in my diary. "Though what those things could have to do with the merit of my book, I cannot say," I wrote.

Of course I called my sister at once, and her first words were, "Now don't get your hopes up, Lou." I said of course I didn't have my hopes up. Which I didn't. Witness the note in my diary: "I feel relatively detached and unexcited. What will come will come."

I told two good friends who came over to discuss the matter with me. After they were gone, I sat down to write the letter Mr. Dodd had asked for.

I said:

Dear Mr. Dodd,
        You have asked me to write a most difficult letter. If you decide against my manuscript—which I realize there is a good chance of your doing—I will always feel it was partly because I said the wrong things in this letter. I feel very much as if I were at the gates of heaven arguing with St. Peter about my entrance requirements.

Then I answered to the best of my ability the questions he had asked me.

This done, I went about my business, teaching my classes as usual. I also gave a talk at a high school assembly in a town some thirty miles from Canyon, and another one to a club in Amarillo. This was a practice smiled upon by college authorities. Good public relations. Lawrence Tibbett came to Amarillo for a concert and several of us went up to hear him. I spent an evening playing duplicate bridge, and I did some Christmas shopping. All in all, pretty much routine stuff.

A week and a day passed by. Then the neighbor who brought our mail to us (there was no delivery in Canyon) came with my mail. In it was a letter from *Redbook*. I sat down hard on one of the great-grandfather chairs in the hall. My hand shook a little as I opened the envelope. I unfolded the sheet, and read what it had to say.

What it had to say was that I had won the Dodd, Mead-*Redbook* award for my novel, *The Years of the Locust*. The presentation would be made in New York, and would I please indicate what date would be convenient for me to come in order that I might receive it in person.

I was alone in the house, my mother being with my sister in Amarillo at the time. I reread the letter just to be sure I had not skipped some vital word. This done, I went to the phone, gave long distance my sister's number. When she answered, I was unable to say a word. I cleared my throat.

"Lou," she said, "what's wrong? You sick or something?"

"I've had a letter," I began, my words getting tangled up like a centipede's legs in a high wind, "I've had a letter . . ." I tried to tell her.

"I can't make a word of sense out of what you're saying," she told me, "but I know it's wonderful. Hold everything—we'll be right down."

She was—with Mama and Bob and a mutual friend and her husband whom Blanche called at once. With them they brought their assorted children and assembled food, for they were cooking dinner at the time. They set the meal on the kitchen table, but I don't know that anyone ate a bite. The phone rang without stopping, and we kept saying how wonderful it all was. Of course Blanche had called a few other friends in Amarillo. And, equally of course, I had told some of my closest friends on the faculty. And naturally, I called my brother and his family in Kansas City. It was all a fine bedlam, especially when people began dropping by to congratulate me. I gravitated between the living room and the telephone like a whirling dervish. This went on for what must have been hours.

One of the faculty members was standing at the door ready to leave when the telephone rang again. He sat down.

"I'm not going until I see who that call's from," he said. "I'm reasonably sure it's President Truman."

It wasn't, of course. But had it been, the call would not

have seemed nearly so wonderful as what had already happened.

Winning the prize was the biggest thing that could have come to me. On the other hand, my condition was one any woman would understand. That was the fall when my clothes had been too good to throw away and not quite smart enough to wear, certainly to wear to New York.

It was also the fall when clothes were not easy to find, with the postwar shortages and all that. Besides, I was teaching much of the day, and shopping requires time. My sister and friends in Amarillo took care of the problem nicely. They divided into squads, one group scouting one side of the main shopping center, another delegation taking the other side. When my last class was finished, I would go to Amarillo and try on what they had found.

Finally, I assembled a wardrobe made up of things I had bought outright, supplemented by items borrowed from my sister and friends. The clerks got in on the excitement, lining up possible items, taking as much interest in the project as if I had belonged personally to them. In a way I did. Down the years they had come to know me well. I had taught many of their children. I was a part of the town.

And all the time, of course, the whole business was supposed to be a secret until the announcement was made at a press conference in New York. In Amarillo, it was about as secret as the noon whistle on a boiler factory. But no matter —the town was sworn to a collective secrecy.

Letters came from New York. One from Mr. Edward Dodd said that doubtless, by now, I knew my "argument with St. Peter had been a success." That, actually, there had never been any question about giving me the prize. They merely

wanted to know a little more about my background and my
letter had taken care of that nicely.

Another letter came from Mr. Balmer, then editor of *Redbook,* and a telegram as well, the latter advising me he was
making a reservation for me at the Algonquin. In all likelihood, someone would meet my train in New York, but if
not, I should go directly to the hotel, and he would get in
touch the next morning.

(Later I was told he was somewhat concerned when he discovered I was a schoolteacher living in Canyon, Texas.

"Where is Canyon?" he asked. "Is it on a railroad? Do you
suppose she can get here if we give her the prize?"

Could I get there! I would have chartered a rocket. I
would have rented a broomstick. Could I get there, indeed!)

I made arrangements for a substitute to take my classes
while I was gone. Mama decided to go as far as Kansas City
with me, and visit my brother and his family while I was in
New York.

The Santa Fe personnel (Amarillo is one of the divisions
for that proud railroad), ruling that nothing short of a drawing room would be suitable for the occasion, had made the
proper arrangements for me. So my mother and I boarded
the train, with the family and well-wishing friends down to
see us off. I had bought a new suit, quite the most beautiful
I have ever owned, and a new fur coat. And, to quote the
sale bills, I also carried with me borrowed items too numer-
ous to mention. (Including a pair of borrowed shoes which
I declared I was afraid to wear lest I lose one of them, like
Cinderella at the ball. The story got around, and thereafter
for some time I was labeled the "Literary Cinderella" of the

writing world. In many ways I felt the title was entirely
justified.)

The train was delayed for hours by a snowstorm. I arrived
in New York sometime in the early morning hours with,
naturally, no one to meet me. I took a taxi to the Algonquin
—I think halfway expected the members of the Round Table
to be waiting there to receive me. Instead, there was only a
bored night clerk who at first had difficulty locating the reservation. I was much later than he had expected, he told me.
I think for a moment he considered saying my room had already been taken. I showed him the telegram which I had
the foresight to bring with me. He looked again. Sure enough,
the room had been reserved. A bellboy showed me to my
room, and I fell into bed. At that moment, I felt lonesome
and letdown.

The next morning brought plenty of calls. A young woman
telephoned from *Redbook*. She thought I might want to do
some shopping, she said, and she would go with me. I said
yes, I would like to buy a dress. And she said, something
else, maybe. And I said, well let's look over what I brought.
If she thought I needed something, I'd buy it.

Once she arrived at my hotel room, I began to bring out
the accumulation—the newly purchased, the borrowed.

"It's exactly right," she would say of each article displayed.
And I would reply, "Yes, we thought it would do."

Finally, she burst out, "I can't get over it—everything you
have is exactly right. Neiman Marcus in Dallas, no doubt?"

"No," I said, "Amarillo, Texas—every one of them."

"Each time I have said something was right, you have

made that same answer," she said. "Who *is* the 'we'—the ones who decided the things were right?"

I gave the matter thought. "My sister," I finally said. "My friends, the saleswomen in Amarillo—well, just about everyone I knew in town, I suppose."

Later I accused the lot of them at both *Redbook* and Dodd, Mead of expecting me—a schoolteacher from a small Western town—to arrive wearing a Mother Hubbard and a sunbonnet. Maybe even spurs, and riding a bronco which I would hitch to the Empire State Building.

They laughed, but did not deny accusation.

I had already been told the award would be given in the presence of members of the press, and afterwards I would have a press conference. This would be a new experience for me. Mr. Balmer, then editor of *Redbook*, and Mr. Bond, then publicity director, later president, of Dodd, Mead, took me to lunch before the occasion.

"The condemned writer at a hearty meal," I quipped. I could joke then, because I really didn't know what lay ahead of me.

Knowledge came the moment we walked into Mr. Balmer's office where the award was to be made. They sat in a rough semicircle, those reporters—three women, three men. All except one of them were on the young side; the older one, a man, was obviously bored. There was also a photographer. The very sight of him made me freeze; I am allergic to photography.

"What do you plan to do with all that money?" one of the girls asked.

They sat, pencils poised, waiting for my answer. Without really saying so, they managed to imply that nobody had a right to take that much money out of New York, back to the hinterlands.

"Well," I said, my voice sounding hollow and strange even to my own ears, "I bought a new dress."

"She bought a new dress," the young reporter next to me wrote on her pad.

"Of course you'll quit teaching now," another said, giving the impression she couldn't care less.

"I'll do nothing of the kind," I flashed back. "I am a teacher. I shall continue teaching. I have no intentions of forsaking the way of life in which I found success."

I felt a stirring of interest in the group.

"I find my work challenging and interesting," I continued. "I thoroughly enjoy the contacts with my fellow teachers and my students. Besides, teachers are needed now with so many G.I.'s coming back after the war is over."

"I suppose you have a great many interesting veterans in your classes," a young man ventured.

"Of course. I also have a great many interesting nonveterans," I said. I considered the matter a moment, and then went on with an observation I had been making rather frequently. "Sometimes I think if we have a lost generation, it will be the boys who were just a little too young to go to war. They sit in the same classes with other boys years older in experience than they are themselves."

The older man leaned forward, aware of me now. I found myself wishing he had stayed in his state of bored remoteness.

"That's the first interesting thing you've said," he told me. "Let me see—are you implying we are doing too much for those students on the G.I. Bill?"

"Wait a minute," I said. I felt real concern now. I could see the headlines, "Author Thinks G.I.'s Are Getting Too Much Consideration." I could anticipate the various patriotic organizations—perhaps even the President—calling to ask for a retraction of my statement. I thought, too, of my own veterans—the ones in my accelerated class as well as those others; the whistle; the young married couples living in the G.I. housing complex; those lonely young ones eating my mother's homemade bread.

"That is not at all what I said," I went on. "I think we are doing no more than we should for the veterans. Those in my classes are my good friends. My own house is sometimes called the Little USO. But at the same time, I think it is important that we not overlook the needs of those students who have not been in service."

"Oh," he said. And that ended his contribution to the press conference.

I could sense a glimmer of interest among the young reporters. Perhaps this was going to be something beyond a routine interview. The brief interchange had given me time to think—to get hold of myself. I took a deep breath.

"You are much like my students," I told them. "You aren't really interested in what I'm saying. You need to ask the questions, though, so you can do your homework."

A few laughs greeted me. Tentative, but nonetheless, laughs. Score one. I leaned forward.

"Listen," I said, "I have never held a press conference before. Obviously, I don't know how to act at one. Let's make a bargain. I'll promise to answer any questions you ask if you, in turn, promise not to make me sound like a fool. Okay?"

The blessed sound of laughter filled the room. Real, spontaneous. The older reporter did not join in it; he leaned
back in his chair, having plainly lost interest. He could see,
there would be no fireworks. The others responded in the
manner of a class that had been given a challenging assignment. They tossed the questions at me like spirited Ping-
pong players. Somehow I fielded the shots; not always with
wisdom or clarity, but I managed. When I faltered occasionally, they helped me. The conference went on and on. Later
I was told that some of them overstayed their time so long
that they had to telephone in their stories.

I was also told, rather a long time afterwards, that Mr.
Bond had come to the conference armed with prepared state-
ments to hand the reporters just in case I flunked the interview. These were not used, but I still wish I might have seen
a copy.

Now it was time to present the checks, one from Dodd,
Mead, one from *Redbook*. I took my place between Mr.
Balmer and Mr. Bond. The photographer stood up. I stiff-
ened.

"Relax," a girl reporter advised. "It won't hurt."

I laughed then, and the photographer's bulb flashed. It
caught Mr. Balmer looking on approvingly while Mr. Bond
handed the check to me, grinning mischievously, and I accused him, acting as if he did not mean to turn loose that
slip of paper after all. When it was over, the photographer
came up to me.

"Maybe you don't know it," he told me, "but I'm from
Dallas—sort of from your neck of the woods, as it were."

"Then," I said, "will you promise to make me look good

in Dallas and Amarillo, and Kansas City, and all the really
important places?"

"I sure nuff will," he assured me.

And he sure nuff did. The picture was highly acceptable.
I came out with all the proper number of eyes and ears and
noses and mouths, and I didn't look even the least bit scared.

There were quieter, yet nontheless rewarding experiences.
Miss Gunterman came by to see me. This was the first time
I had met the woman with whom I had worked on my two
books for young people. It was like having a reunion with
someone whom I had long known. Naturally, Dr. Jewett,
who had guided my progress in Teachers College, and Miss
Brewster, who had played a big part in my writing career,
got in touch with me, and in each case we were able to ar-
range a satisfying visit together.

The mother of one of my students from New York City
came to the hotel to call on me, bearing a gift. Her son was
a good student, and came often to my house.

There was another meeting, no less interesting—and yes,
in a way, a reunion of sorts. We used *The Saturday Review*
in our English classes, as did many colleges. Always, we
turned first to "Trade Winds," then written by Bennett
Cerf, president of Random House. I had asked my young
substitute if there was any small token I could bring her
from New York as an additional offering. She said, yes, an
autographed copy of Mr. Cerf's most recent book. So, when
Mr. Howard Lewis, of Dodd, Mead, asked me if there was
anything more I wanted to do before leaving New York, I
said I'd like to see Bennett Cerf.

He seemed to think the request an extremely funny one.
Immediately he had Mr. Cerf on the line. "Bennett," he said,

"we have a prize-winning novelist here with what I think is a very mistaken request. She wants to see you."

The reply was evidently satisfactory, for almost before I knew it I was in a taxi headed for Random House. Mr. Cerf treated me with the utmost consideration. I departed with not one but two autographed copies of his book—one for my substitute, one for myself. Later he wrote about me in "Trade Winds," calling me a "beguiling young lady." Of the several definitions of the word, naturally I chose to accept the most flattering one.

There were other events of interest.

When the news stories about the prize came out, almost everyone of them used, in some variation or other, these words, "She'll stick to teaching." Scarcely had the papers hit the stands when my telephone started ringing.

Reader's Digest was on the phone. Did I mean what I said about sticking to teaching? I was crisp. I was not in the habit of saying things I did not mean, I retorted.

If I did mean it, would I write an article telling them why I had made this decision?

I think perhaps I was a little giddy. Or maybe I even thought it was not the *Digest* at all, but, rather someone trying to play a trick on me.

"I'll have to think about it," I said.

The voice on the other end of the line sounded a bit incredulous.

"You mean. . . ."

"I mean," I said, gathering courage, "I'll think about it. Listen—I've written two highly successful and significant books about teaching and you did not even notice them, much as we tried to get you to do so. Now, when something happens which has little connection with teaching, you're on my trail. I still say I'll think about it."

"Well," he said, "we might not take it, even if you write it. You realize that."

"I might not write it," I retorted.

He hung up. So did I. All the time I meant to do that article. I was like a girl running away, looking over her shoulder to be sure the boy was following her.

I did write the article titled, appropriately enough, "I'll Stick To Teaching." The *Digest* printed it. Later it was reissued in pamphlet form, along with other articles and stories intended to inspire young people to go into the profession.

The inevitable calls came in—people wanting me to help them with their books or help revise ones already written, or assist them in interesting an agent in their writing. (The last request was easy to answer. I had sold *The Years of the Locust* myself, without an agent's help. Some of them didn't believe me, and said so.) Photographers called, wanting to take my picture. (One of them did.) Agents called or wrote, wanting to represent me. I disposed of these in short order— all except one.

Annie Laurie Williams, having read the newspaper stories, came to the Algonquin to see me. Her husband, Maurice Crain, was originally from Canyon, Texas, she said. His parents, brother, and family still lived there. Naturally, she was interested in me as a person as well as a prospective client. Although by this time both Dodd, Mead and I had received several requests to represent me on the movie rights, I chose Annie Laurie Williams as my agent.

I went back to Texas, stopping in Kansas City to pick up

my mother, and to visit with my brother and his wife and their young daughter, Elizabeth Ann, and various other kin and friends.

"Lulie," my brother told me, once the greetings were over, "some gal from the *Star* has been calling. She wants to do a story about you. Said she'd call back."

She did, just as I was leaving for the beauty shop.

"Why don't we meet there?" she suggested.

I said that made sense, and then I did a quick double take. "But no picture," I decreed firmly. I wasn't about to be photographed under a dryer. "I'll bring one I had made in New York," I promised.

She agreed. When I arrived at the beauty shop, she was already there waiting for me. We had a pleasant time talking together, and before long, she went off with the picture and the story. The next morning, even before I was up, Elizabeth Ann called to me.

"Lou!" she cried, "you're on the front page! Picture, too."

There was reason for her excitement.

When I was growing up and, to a certain degree, even to this day, we lived and died by the Kansas City *Star* and its morning edition, the *Times.* If we failed to read about an event in one of those papers, we didn't quite believe it really happened. I think we were all halfway convinced that the ultimate earthly reward of a long and good and self-sacrificing life was a four-line obit on the back page of the *Star* or *Times.*

Now here I was on the front page, with picture. And I was still alive.

Mama and I went back to Amarillo. Friends and family met the train, including one student who had just sold an article.

I came down the train steps asking facetiously, "Where are the photographers? I've been having my picture made everywhere but standing on my head in Times Square."

At that moment, one of them popped up from behind a reporter. I felt like a fool.

Amarillo, too, had front page stories and pictures. Friends rallied round and it was all dear and wonderful and heartwarming beyond any telling.

The Panhandle Pen Women, an organization to which I still belong, honored me with a dinner. Various testimonials were given me at the program which followed the meal. By my sister, by fellow writers, by students. The one I remember best was a part of the remarks by a man who had at one time been my principal.

"Out at our school," he said, "we would have come to a dinner for Lou even if she had never written a book."

That's the spirit. Your friends are going to like you anyway, with or without benefit of book.

Chapter Six

One of the questions Mr. Edward Dodd, then vice-president of Dodd, Mead, had asked in the letter he wrote before the awarding of the prize was whether I planned to continue writing. Of course I said I did. While I was in New York to receive the award, I had a short conference with him.

"Do you have another book in mind?" he asked.

"Well . . . yes, . . ." I said hesitatingly.

"What is it about?"

I sketched the idea. He did not seem overly impressed, but then I am never good at talking ahead of time about something I mean to write.

"We all hope you'll give us another one soon," he said.

"I'll try," I assured him, filing his words away in my memory so I could write in my diary that evening, "Dodd, Mead asked for another book."

I think I saw him somewhat in the role of a teacher who had given me an assignment. Best I get busy with my homework right away. This was a new experience for me. Although Miss Gunterman was pleased and helpful above and beyond the call of duty with my second teaching book, she herself had not set me to writing it. Rather, the suggestion had come from teachers and others in the education field. Now that Dodd, Mead had made the request, I felt I had no other choice. Especially since it was what I meant to do anyway.

In fact, I had every intention of going back to Texas and whipping out another book as fast as I could lay finger to typewriter. Only that's not quite the way things worked out.

Something there is about a prize novel which seems to capture the imagination of the public. Other books, even those by the same author, may be better or more widely read; reviewers may (and often do) take a dim view of them or, if approving, express astonishment that a prize novel can still be good. In general, though, people remember the prize winning book and forever after associate it with the author.

The details of the award for *The Years of the Locust*, together with my picture, were printed around the world. Almost immediately letters began to pour in. From former students, some of them still in distant countries with the armed forces; from relatives and friends and acquaintances, many of whom I had not seen or heard of for years; from complete strangers. A woman in Portugal wrote what practically amounted to a threat. No woman, she told me, had a right to that much money. She, the writer, was in a state of dire distress and unless I sent her a generous gift at once she would visit some sort of vengeance on me. The nature of this visitation was vague, but as nearly as I could gather, it amounted to a hex. There were many letters frankly begging in nature also coming from all over the world.

And, without end, people wanting me to help them with a book in progress, give information about agents and publishers, or co-author a book with them. One man wrote to confide that he knew about a secret buried in the basement of the place where he lived, and if I would only help him escape, he would share it with me. The secret, he assured me, would make a best seller.

The letter came from a mental institution.

There were also proposals of marriage, and, of course, countless bargains offered me, from lots in Florida to stock in gold mines.

Everybody, or so it seemed, wanted me to speak. There is no necessary correlation between good speaking and good writing, but once a book is published, the author is besieged with requests to give talks in all sorts of places on every imaginable subject. I accepted more than reason or judgment would have indicated I should. Once when it was necessary for me to go to another state for an appearance, my brother was firm with me.

"You can't afford to run all over the country," he told me. "That mounts up into real money."

"Oh," I reassured him, "they're paying me."

"I can't get over it," he marveled, shaking his head in unbelief. "People paying you now to talk when any old day in my life I would have paid you to shut your mouth!"

We both agreed he had a point.

I had said at my press conference in New York that I had no intentions of changing my way of life because I had written a prize novel. Essentially, I kept my word. I carried a full teaching load. I continued to have a great deal of company, much of it the drop-in kind. Fortunately, less is expected of a hostess when she is taken by surprise. In rechecking my diary for those busy months I often find this record: "So-and-so dropped by this afternoon. Stayed on for a meal of sorts."

The "meal of sorts" would sometimes be leftovers. Or scrambled eggs or canned soup with a salad. And always Mama's homemade bread which could rescue any meal.

There is a very special quality to life in a college community. It is a world in itself, one which makes its own laws and then enforces them; sets its own standards and pretty well abides by them; defines its own boundaries and stays within them. In a way, it is deeply provincial. But it is also a place of mind and spirit, unlimited in scope, moving freely not only in the whole wide world but in the infinite space above and around it as well.

Especially is this true in the case of a smaller school in a town where there is a happy blending of Town and Gown, as was the case in Canyon. I belonged to a dinner-discussion club with members from both groups. The range of topics touched upon and the breadth of knowledge displayed by those who led and those who participated in the discussions proved truly phenomenal.

There were also friendly get-togethers among the faculty members themselves, and sometimes small informal dinner parties. A faculty party always has a certain flair, an *élan*. The menu may be very simple (especially just before payday), but even so, the host and hostess have a way of making the party an occasion.

Of course, there were concerts and plays and lectures, the

latter occasionally given by some celebrity we had been able
to lure to our campus. Sometimes these visitors would be
people I knew, in which case I would ask them to come by
the Pueblo, at the same time suggesting to my students that
they also drop by to say hello. They came, filling all the
available chairs and when the supply was exhausted, sitting
on cushions on the floor. Upon one of these occasions, a
young student said, "I don't understand why the walls of this
little house don't push right off the foundations. All the big
talk that goes on here."

Big talk did, indeed, go on.

Once having formed the habit, students continued coming,
even when no visitor was present. They borrowed books. They
sat and talked. Some of them even brought their dates. (An
excellent way to spend the evening. Bread and jelly and
cookies and help with homework. All for free. What more
could you ask for!) One evening a few of them came by with
one of Shakespeare's plays they were currently studying in
class. "Here, listen to this, . . ." a student said, beginning to
read a portion aloud. After that, the practice was continued.
I can see the picture now—students sitting in the little living
room, either reading or listening, or breaking in with questions or comments. My mother also listening, knitting needles
flashing in and out. She was delighted—company, no matter
what brought them, was a joy to her. I had some reservations.
Interesting as these sessions often proved, they did pretty well
use up an evening.

And I needed these evenings. For one thing, I had discovered that I could take my rejected stories, revise a bit,
and send them off. Frequently I made a sale. Perhaps I knew
more about writing now, although I suspect the real reason

was that my name looked better in the table of contents since I had won the prize. Whatever the explanation, I was gratified at the sale.

And of course there was the book I had promised Mr. Dodd I would write. The book I myself wanted to write.

Before I had time to give it more than a thought, however, the spring semester started and I walked into my newly enrolled evening class to find it full and running over. I suppose some of the increase was due to the publicity attendant on my receiving the prize. If I could work that sort of magic in my own behalf, perhaps I might be able to pass part of it on, they may have reasoned.

Not only was the class large, but it also represented a wide variety of people. There were grandmothers and college students; junior league members and businessmen and women; teachers and a cook in a cafe; published writers and rank amateurs.

Almost at the beginning of the class a built-in radar type of instinct told me that I had two problem students. One was a young boy, tall, taciturn, obviously bored with the whole business. The other problem was a woman. I have since come to recognize her type, someone for whom writing is a sort of daydream, a record of wishful thinking, a substitute for a life which for one reason or another has become unbearable. A rope of words, as it were, to pull herself out of a well of despair. At the time, I realized only there was a difficulty without being able to name it.

She was attractive in a vague, haunting way, married—or so I was told—to a man her friends and family thought beneath her. She approached writing as a person long on an enforced diet would fall upon food. Each week she came to

class with a new story; or rather, the same story with new
character names and a different setting.

All were identical in theme. Always the heroine was a
woman so irresistibly beautiful that wherever she went—
and all of them traveled widely—every man in sight promptly
fell at her feet. Old ones, young ones, the in-betweens. Every
one of the men had in common two things: great wealth
and complete awareness of the heroine's charms.

After some half dozen of these stories, I realized the class
had had enough—quite enough—and everyone was wondering
why I did not put an end to the nonsense. I, too, was fed
up, but I was also in a quandary. I had announced at the
very beginning that, in my class, people wrote what they
wanted to, not assignments I gave them or themes upon
which I looked with approval. Even so, I knew she had to be
stopped, one way or another. Finally, I ventured the comment that her stories were lacking in suspense. Surely somewhere, sometime, there would be a man—one lone individual
—who would not succumb to the heroine's charms, if for
nothing more than variety's sake.

She looked at me as if I had just voiced the great sacrilege.

"Oh, Miss Erdman," she said, with conscious superiority,
"how could you possibly know about such things, since you
never have been married or anything?"

The young boy lifted himself at least two inches off his
shoulder blades, where he had been sitting until now, and
came forth with the one observation of his class career.

"How can you be so sure about that *anything* business?" he
asked gruffly.

The class, and I, sat silent for a moment. Then they, and I,
as if by prearrangement, broke into laughter—spontaneous,

unrestrained. By the time it subsided, no one felt the need to answer either his question or hers. The boy lapsed back into his habitual silence; it was not long afterwards that he dropped the class. The woman wrote fewer stories, and those she did write were of a different type altogether.

The incident confirmed my earlier convictions. With the right conditions and a good opportunity, the members of the class will give more valid criticism than can be achieved if the teacher alone is the final judge. It's the old English idea of justice—a jury of one's peers is capable of arriving at a fair verdict.

Any teacher knows quite well that not every one of her students will become a recognized authority in the subject matter with which the class deals. This is especially true in a writing class. Inevitably the books of only a few members will appear in print. But there are other gains beyond that of having a piece of writing published, desirable as that may be. No one expects every person who takes art lessons to have a picture hanging in some recognized art gallery; certainly music lessons do not guarantee that the ones who have them will perform in a symphony or on a concert stage. These people do, however, understand and appreciate art and music a little more because they have studied about them.

This same fact holds true for a writing class. Its members will, because of their study of the structure and style and craft of writing, be able to understand all writing better. There are other gains as well, ones we might well term therapeutic. For instance, the class discussion is good. Perhaps it was even a healthy thing for the woman to set her daydreams down. The act of doing so may have served as a tranquilizer of sorts, and in this age of tranquilizers, we should welcome one which has no harmful side effects and is, in all probability, nonlethal. The only drawback could be, so far as women are concerned, that they pile the dishes in the sink and, with men, that they fail to mow the lawn on schedule.

In this particular class there were tangible results, expressed by two women, both of whom, as the Episcopalians so aptly put it, were "of riper years."

There was one woman who, I thought, should not be in the class at all. I was considering having a conference with her, suggesting that she drop the course instead of remaining for the failing grade which seemed inevitable. Even as I was planning how best to break the news to her, she handed in a piece of writing with a note attached to it. The note read as follows:

"I can't write worth a hoot. I know it and you know it. But don't feel sorry for me, and don't try to get me to drop the course. I go home evenings after this class so happy I can't sleep. I'm part of a group. Someone has listened to me. For the first time in my life, someone listened. I say what I really think, deep inside me. And you all listen. Hear me? You listen. And just about the time the glow wears off, it's class night again, and I come back and it starts all over. Don't be worried because I don't say things right, or flowery, or the way real writers do. You just keep on listening and let the others listen, too."

I gave no more thought to having her drop the class.

Another woman said, "I started this evening class because my husband and children were college graduates. I had barely finished high school. I felt they were leaving me behind, and I was determined to do something about it. The first few sessions, I was almost too scared to answer when you called the roll. Now, after six weeks of it, I'd spit in a rattlesnake's eye if one happened to take a notion to crawl in the door."

Fortunately, no rattlesnakes appeared, but I have no doubt she would have done just as she promised had one showed up.

It was under these circumstances that I began the book I had promised Mr. Dodd I would write.

The writing was far from easy. Too many things were crowding in on me. I was pulled in too many directions. I think this is often the case with women writers. Somewhere I read that the reason so few women become great writers is that they have no wives. This might well be true. Most of the men writers I know (Mr. Shakespeare notwithstanding) have wives who protect their privacy; who run the homes; who answer the phone and stand between their writer husbands and most of the nagging details of daily life—such as unexpected callers and door-to-door salesmen. They cook the meals and keep the clothes in order, and maybe even balance the checkbook and pay the bills. Women who write do most of these things in addition to writing. As I often say, "Men write; women also write." As indeed they do. Women, more often than not, merely add writing to all their other duties. And somehow, they manage.

In this connection I like to relate an experience which came to me in my early Pueblo days. I was sitting at the typewriter, feeling pleased to have the words flowing so smoothly. The weather was warm; my back door was open.

Suddenly, I heard a succession of wild screams—surely some child had been captured by the Indians, or was being hotly pursued by starving wolves. The screams arrived at my own back door; a little neighbor girl jerked open the screen and rushed in. She had, it seemed, fallen and cut her knee. At least six drops of blood testified to the fact.

I administered the necessary first aid, together with a cookie. Then, the emergency over, I reacted as mothers are said to do when their children's hurts are less severe than had been indicated at first. I began to shake from fear, and something between anger and impatience. Obviously I couldn't spank the child, but I could reprimand her.

"Why didn't you go to your mother?" I asked. My voice had nothing of sweetness or light in it.

"Because, . . ." she lifted big blue eyes, beginning once more to fill with tears. "Because *you were closest.*"

That is the pattern for most women writers. They are closest to the interruptions and duties and various activities which must go on. I accepted her explanation; I still do.

I knew I was writing too hastily. I myself was not satisfied with what I did. But then, what writer ever is, I tried to tell myself. I had known great moments of doubt and even despair while writing my other books. In time I would come up with something acceptable. The main thing was to keep trying.

Writing now was certainly not easy. I was nervous and tired and showed the strain. It brought back to me a memory of an incident in the early days of my writing, after a few of my stories had come out under my own name in papers read by most of the people in the community where I grew up.

I was home for summer vacation and had a cold. I was not sick enough to call the doctor (a drastic step in a small town). Instead, I went to his office for medicine and advice. While I waited for my father to pick me up and take me back home, a woman came into the office. Life had not been easy for her—hard work and many children and a husband who fell far short of what she might have wished him to be. I saw her watching me, checking my lack of makeup, my general run-down condition. Finally she spoke.

"You are Loula Grace Erdman, aren't you?" she asked.

I said, yes, I was.

She looked at me a long time, silently taking stock. I felt myself squirming under her direct, unblinking gaze.

"Well," she finally broke the silence. "They say that gittin' married and workin' hard and havin' a bunch of kids is hard on a woman. But I must say that stayin' single and writin' stories ain't done much for you!"

A quick and entirely fitting retort crowded to my lips. Fortunately, I did not give it voice. Suddenly I could see how her own life, which at times must have seemed hopeless, now became a little more bearable. Not willingly would I deny this compensation to anyone, even though it is realized at my expense. I was not being noble and great-souled; rather, I realized dimly something which I have now come to see with greater clarity and understanding. Perhaps here was part of the contribution writing has to make, both to those who read and the ones who write. A certain perspective. An easing, just a little, of the pressures of life by giving added insight and meaning. Making sense and order where, before, there had been doubt and chaos.

However, I was entertaining no such philosophical thoughts during this busy summer after I had returned from New York. Rather, I was thinking that writing wasn't doing one thing for me, mostly because I wasn't doing any writing. I told myself I was too busy, that too many things were crowding in on me. As, indeed, they were. For one thing, I had bought a car. My first. Until now, I had scarcely so much as had my hands on a steering wheel.

My knowledge of things mechanical is sub-zero, a fact recognized by my family and friends alike. This can be best illustrated by a story, still told by members of my family. Once when we were making ready to take off on some jaunt or other, someone thoughtfully suggested we better check the state of the tires. The further suggestion was that I, being closest to the door, undertake the task.

"Oh, no," Bill spoke up. Bill was the double cousin, reared in our home and loved like a brother, a status which gave him the brotherly prerogative of frankness to the sisters in the family. "Oh, no," he protested. "Don't send Lulie. She wouldn't know if all four wheels were off."

It was a judgment which had not changed down the years, and one evidently shared by my students who now looked darkly on any attempt on my part to clutter up the roads. When word got around that I had bought a car and was in the process of learning to herd the thing along, a group visited me.

"We'll teach you to drive," they volunteered without en-thusiasm, the implication being that their offer was made not so much for my sake as to ensure their own safety, once I began contributing to traffic hazards.

"Yes, we taught her to drive," they say now. "Ninety miles an hour on the Canyon Highway."

There was, of course, an element of exaggeration in the

statement. But they did teach me to drive as they drove—
without fear, automatically.

"Shall I try to pass that car?" I asked timidly. An old man
in an ancient vehicle was just ahead, going, perhaps, twenty
miles an hour.

"Unless you want to camp out on the highway," they said.
"Listen—a slow car is a greater menace on the highway than
a fast one. Whip on around."

I whipped.

In the fall, *The Years of the Locust* publication date arrived, with considerable fanfare in Amarillo. Reviews came.
Almost every one was good; some of them were even semi-
raves. At the time I think I took them pretty much for
granted, assuming that all books received this treatment. If
I remember correctly, there were two unfavorable ones. I
evidently did not even bother to keep them, for they are
not in the scrapbook with the other clippings. One, as I
recall, amounted almost to a personal attack. Mr. Bond wrote
me, trying to soften the blow. I replied with what I thought
then, and what I still believe. Everyone has a right to think
what he wants about any book he reads, including mine.
Equally, I have a right to think his opinion is completely mistaken and greatly misguided.

Who is to say there is only one type of good literature,
either to read or to write? That is an attitude for a writer or
a reader in a totalitarian country, but not for us who consider free speech a part of our heritage and book banning
something to raise our fears.

The Years of the Locust was a book club choice. It made
the best seller list. True, it was well toward the bottom, and
did not stay long, but still, it was there. It was translated into

many languages. (The artist's conception of a Missouri farmer on the jacket of the Arabic edition is something to see.) It has been transcribed into Braille. After twenty-one years, it is still in print, and has recently been picked up by paperbacks. I frequently get letters from people who have just read it for the first time and want to tell me how much they liked it.

I finished *Lonely Passage* in the early spring after *The Years of the Locust* was published. I sent the manuscript to Dodd, Mead. In April, I went Washington, there to address the National Pen Women, since I was at that time a member of the Kansas City Chapter of which the National President, Mrs. Alma Robinson Higbee, was also a member. She knew Mrs. Truman. It was only natural under the circumstances that Mrs. Truman would have the group at the White House for tea.

Two incidents of that meeting are forever engraved in my mind and heart. One, the organization presented me with a small gold locket in the shape of a book. I still wear it. The other was concerned with the White House tea.

"Bess," Mrs. Higbee said, "I want you to meet Loula Grace Erdman. She wrote——"

"I know," Mrs. Truman said. "She wrote *The Years of the Locust*. I have read it once; it's on my bedside table, and I'm reading it a second time. Next week, when we go home, I'm taking it for Harry to read."

I thought—Missouri is "home" to her, as, in a way, it is to me. She may not still remember the incident, but I do. Not just as it concerns me, but as a manifestation of graciousness and thoughtfulness which we like to associate with our First Ladies. A very charming woman, Bess Wallace Truman.

From Washington I went on to New York. By now, I felt a sense of homecoming when I went to the Dodd, Mead office. I am afraid I never stood back on protocol there. Then, as now, I popped in, often without being properly announced, wandering down the hall (at that time they were in the old building on Fourth Avenue) and various ones came out of their offices to chat with me. My relations with my publishers have always been most cordial. They are my friends. Some authors hint darkly that publishers—all of them—are up to no good. I have always trusted mine, proceeding on the thesis that what is good for them is also good for me.

Certainly this visit now was nothing like my first trip. No prize this time, no press conference. I hadn't expected either, but even so there was a—well—a letdown feeling. I think this came largely from a growing suspicion in my mind. Namely, they were not enthusiastic about the manuscript I had sent ahead. Nothing was put into words, but I felt the implication. Like a mother who sees her child rejected when the rejection is a thing of spirit rather than of words or action.

"You don't like this new book," I said to Mr. Bond.

"I didn't say that," he told me. "We are planning to publish it in the fall, as you know."

"But you don't like it," I insisted.

"Well . . ." he hedged. "It's really a sad little book," he added.

I looked up quickly, wondering if he meant "sad" in the connotation my students used the word.

"I don't mean sad in the sense of being poor," he explained. "Rather, that it arouses a vague feeling of sadness when one reads it."

I knew what he meant. Because the book was concerned mostly with young people, there was sadness. This was not surprising. I had been thrown with young people a great deal during the past two years. I had listened to them as they, either consciously or unconsciously, revealed the stories of their own lives. Some of these revelations were touched with sadness. Youth is not a time of unalloyed joy.

The day before I left, Mr. Bond took me to lunch.

"Why don't you try a book on Texas next?" he suggested.

I remember thinking, gratefully, that *Lonely Passage* must be better than I had halfway feared or he wouldn't be suggesting I write another book.

"Oh," I protested, "I don't know a thing about ranches."

At the time, I thought, as is still the case with many people all over the world, the words "Texas" and "ranch" were synonymous.

"You can read, can't you?" he pointed out. "You can do research. You can look around. You can ask questions. After all, you are sitting in the middle of the ranch country."

Which was true. As I remember, I made some sort of half promise to think about his suggestion.

We went our separate ways, he to his office, I to my hotel room to pack and organize things before leaving. And, almost unconsciously, to begin the thinking I had promised to do. My other books for Dodd, Mead had stemmed from a background I knew well, had required no research at all. If I wrote the Texas book I would be moving into relatively unfamiliar territory. I would need help from people who were authorities on the history of the region and the period in which I would set my story. If, indeed, I decided to do it.

I took my first step in this direction by asking Maurice

Crain, Annie Laurie Williams' husband and himself a native Texan, if he would act as my agent.

"Do you have an idea in mind?" he asked.

"Yes—" I said hesitantly. "At least, I think I do."

"And it is?"

"Something about Texas—set in the Panhandle ranch country."

"Well," he told me, "at least you won't have to travel far to get your material."

Even so, I was not sure about the idea. I went back to Texas, without committing myself one way or another. And, as usual, I found myself being busy with many things.

Lonely Passage was published in the fall. It found its own place. The newly formed Christian Herald's Family Bookshelf used it as the initial selection. It went into several foreign languages. A former student found a copy in, of all places, a bookstore in North Africa. It was transcribed into Braille. The book has been out of print for some time now, but recently a church group used a portion in a study manual for the junior high school age group. I discovered this quite by accident and was moved to write the editor who had compiled the manual to ask what factors had been involved in making the selection. He replied that the woman responsible for the choice had been favorably influenced by the book, feeling it opened up new dimensions of loneliness. Naturally I was pleased. If only one person remembered and drew comfort from a book, it had reason for being. Of course we hope for a wider audience, but one is better than none.

Anyway, writers must face the fact that few authors blaze forth like meteors, shining bright for all the world to see. Most of us are destined to light a small lantern which, hope-

fully, will illuminate an area of human experience, a segment of time, a bit of history, a portion of a region, and in
so doing, help people to understand each other and themselves a little better. Therein lies both the responsibility and
the reward of those who manipulate words. And, just as a
ray of light cannot be called back once it has left its source,
so a published book is out of an author's hands. No matter
how much we might like to control its destiny, we are unable
to do so.

I suspect there is no author who has not at one time or
another felt disappointment or frustration or any one of a
host of emotions at seeing a book of his own, or of a friend,
or even of someone he does not know, miss out on a coveted
honor or recognition while one which seemed (to him) less
worthy has succeeded. He may lay this to poor timing or
lack of advertising or luck or mistaken judgment on the part
of those who made the decision. But whatever the reason, a
writer must learn to take things the way they come.

A most excellent training in self-discipline, this writing
business.

The real discipline of writing, however, does not come
from learning to take disappointments, necessary as that may
be. It is the by-product of writing itself. Not dreaming about
writing, or talking about it, or telling people (or yourself)
that next week, without fail, you are going to sit down at the
typewriter and start something. Knowing this, I decided I
had given quite enough time to thinking about my next
book. Now I would begin the writing. And I would follow
the suggestion made by Dodd, Mead and have a try at a book
set in the Panhandle of Texas.

Chapter Seven

Originally I had come to Texas from the University of Wisconsin. My roommate, Victoria Warner, had been born and reared in the Texas Panhandle, that portion of the state which sticks up on the map like a chimney on a house. The picture I had of Amarillo, the principal city in this sizable hunk of land, did not come from anything she told me but, rather, from the western movies I had seen, the western novels I had read.

I envisioned a smallish group of people huddled in an ocean of ranches. The town's boundaries were marked by hitchracks to which tall soft-spoken cowboys tied their horses before lounging into the local saloons in order to indulge in a few innocent capers like shooting at tenderfeet to see them jump. Over the scene ranchers reigned—benign, generous, and immensely rich—all wearing Stetson hats and high-heeled boots.

Victoria's mother, Mrs. Phebe K. Warner, herself a nationally known writer and clubwoman, came to Madison to visit her daughter. She and I liked each other on sight. When she suggested I come to Amarillo to teach, I agreed it was an excellent idea, and how about my sister coming too. Mrs. Warner agreed that was an excellent idea. Amarillo was growing fast and the school system needed teachers.

That fall my sister and I went to Amarillo to begin teaching there. We did not find the movie-set sort of place I had halfway expected, or told myself I had. Instead, there was a bustling little city which seemed larger than its actual size since it served such a large trade territory. True, it was set in a level expanse of land, but one scarcely got out of town before coming to a very different terrain—to the north and east, the breaks of the Canadian River; to the south, the Palo Duro Canyon.

The cowboys were there, although I believe it was rather a longish time before I saw one I knew to be the genuine article. The ranchers were there, too, wearing big hats as I had anticipated. But bankers and oil men also wore them, as did insurance salesmen and drugstore clerks and merchants and farmers.

Colonel Goodnight, who had driven his herds down from Colorado and who, with his wife, had been the first white settler in the Panhandle, was still alive. In his late nineties, he was a vigorous and commanding old gentleman. I myself shook hands with him once, feeling dimly as I did so that the present was reaching out living hands to touch the past. Many other early settlers were still alive. Fortunately, the region was history conscious and pioneers were either writing down their own memoirs or telling them to others who in turn recorded them. Over the years many of these had been preserved in the Panhandle Plains Historical Museum, housed on the campus at Canyon where I now taught.

I even had some of these old-timers in my writing classes. One, a retired minister, I shall never forget.

He had come to this region a long time ago, he told us. Walking, in a country where no one walked. He was a traveling preacher, and if he were to do his work, he must have a horse. He asked the Lord to help him find one, and the Lord guided him to a certain ranch. Once there, he stated his need.

"I have ten dollars to pay for a horse," he told the cowboys. "I need it in order to do the Lord's work."

The cowboys looked at each other and then at him.

"Got one over there you can have for nothing—if you can ride him," they told the preacher.

Sure enough, there stood a horse off by himself, black as night and big and rangy. Ideal for the long distances the preacher must cover. He went over to touch the horse and it drew back like a wild animal.

The class was listening now as the preacher continued, relating details. How the horse had been cruelly treated by the man who set out to break him; how, even now, his mouth was so bruised and sore he had found it difficult to drink and impossible to eat. The minister patted him gently, coaxed him to the tank where he drank deeply. Once the horse had slaked his thirst, the preacher turned to the cowboys.

"All right," he said, "I'll ride him now."

They were backing down.

"Preacher," they said, "better not try. He's a Devil, that one."

"Daily, I'm accustomed to wrestling with the Devil," the preacher told them. "With the Lord's help, I'll manage."

He did, but not before he had banished all the watching cowboys. He discovered they were laying bets as to his probable success.

"And once I gentled him," the preacher finished his story, "the Devil and I, we rode all over the Panhandle of Texas, doing the Lord's work."

"Write it," I urged him. "Just the way you told us."

"Oh, no," he said gently. "That would be writing about myself. I want to tell about the people I ministered to. Special people. Those who settled this country."

The old preacher went on to his eternal reward before he set down the story of those "special people." Now, as I began the research for my book, it was almost as if he had left the job to me. I cannot say I felt either willing or capable, but nonetheless I started.

Another older student, a woman, told a poignant story with no drama such as the preacher had displayed and almost no emotion. It concerned her first baby who had died. She wasn't going to have it buried out here, where if any words were said they'd have to say them themselves. And, afterwards, pile rocks over the little grave to keep the coyotes from digging it up. She made her young husband drive her back to town, "Where there were people" lying in a cemetery, the way things ought to be.

Another story had stayed on my mind—one about a woman who planted a rosebush beside her dugout and fought drouth and wind and blizzard to keep it alive. I could understand this. When my mother's grandmother came from Virginia, she had brought with her a cutting from a "maiden blush" rosebush, one whose flowers were faintly flushed with pink. The rosebush thrived. My mother had one in our own garden, a cutting from the original Virginia bush. My sister brought a cutting from our home to Texas and planted it in her own yard.

Against this background of information I began my reading in the files at the Panhandle Plains Historical Museum. Boone McClure, the curator, himself an inexhaustible source of information about the country as well as the museum's material, helped me. I lost myself in the history of the region as told by the people who had lived it.

The figure of the cowboy naturally loomed large in those memoirs I read. In the Panhandle, however, there had been no rancher-homesteader feud, a situation which has become almost a cliché in western stories and movies. True, the nester was not welcome—building his fences, plowing under the grass the Lord meant the cattle to eat, and generally cluttering up the landscape. But the ranchers realized his coming was inevitable, especially after the passage of the Homestead Act.

Little as Colonel Goodnight wanted these nesters, he was still kind and understanding. A man who knew him well said the old gentleman frequently rode over to have a first-hand look at a newly arrived homesteader family. If they appeared sturdy and substantial, and if there were children —and especially if the wife looked like a hard worker and a good woman—he would tell them he had a milk cow who was eating her head off and if they wanted to feed her they could keep her that winter. Cowboys would not have been caught dead milking a cow but they were not a bit above dropping by the nester's dugout for a meal which included butter and buttermilk. Homesteader wives knitted socks and wristlets and scarves for the cowboys, earning for themselves what was often the only cash money the family had. Many homesteader children were clothed in garments made from shirts the cowboys handed over to the mothers. "Shucks, this ain't no good—take it and make the kids something."

It is no wonder that in the retelling of the stories the cowboy has become larger than life. This is also true of the West itself, of which the Texas Panhandle is a part. It has become a sort of Never-Never-Land which did not exist, at least in the way people want to believe it did. A bit of wistful thinking. A dream living in the hearts of little boys playing Cowboys and Indians; a later Grail beckoning adolescents who harbored visions of great deeds they would do; a fantasy set down by writers who had never been west of the Hudson.

The romanticists held fast to this West they were sure they knew, peopling it with valiant men who performed heroic deeds and then rode back to pure and noble women. Good was always recognizable and evil was unfailingly punished. It was, actually, the essence of the dream of America, a place where every man was free to work out his own destiny and be rewarded according to his desserts. If the West did not exist, it should have, so people set about concocting it. And because every dream must have a setting, they placed it on a ranch just as the dream of chivalry, also necessary to the mind of man, was anchored in a feudal castle or in Camelot.

And I, who had grown up believing in the fiction I had read about the West, had now set myself to studying those people who had really lived it.

A friend in the northern part of the Panhandle thought I could get some interesting information from her father-in-

law who had been an early settler in the region. I drove up
one Sunday in June.

Yes, he had pioneered here, the old gentleman told me.
He and his wife were both young, and they had three children. Her brother came with them and he, too, claimed a
section of land and built a dugout. They plowed up some
land with a sodbuster and planted row crops. They had a
pretty good work team, and the old gentleman—who wasn't
old then, by any means—had a good riding horse.

One day he drove his wagon over in order to get water
from a neighboring rancher. (That was the added humiliation—all too often the homesteaders had to ask the ranchers
for water.) On his way home, he saw a prairie fire headed in
his direction. He knew his only safety lay in outrunning it,
but he realized this was impossible, for the wind was blowing
the fire straight toward him at a speed greater than the team
could travel, slowed down as they were by the wagon and
its load of water. He did the only possible thing under the
circumstances. He cut the horses loose, trusting them to find
their way home. Then he crawled under the wagon, thinking
to let the fire burn over him, hoping the wagon would be
protection enough to save his life.

"I had been a pretty wicked man," he told me. "You know
how young fellows are. I smoked and I drank and I cussed
a little. But as I lay under that wagon, watching the fire
racing toward me, I promised the Lord if he'd save me I'd
never smoke or drink or say another cuss word as long as I
lived."

The team started toward the dugout, running as if their
lives depended on it, as indeed they did. The fire came. It
burned over the wagon, which gave some protection to the

old gentleman. He was burned, but not fatally. When he felt it was safe to do so, he crawled out from his refuge and hobbled home. His wife treated his burns with coal oil and lard, the standard home remedy of the time.

"I got well," he said. "But do you know what? My brother-in-law couldn't take it. The fire just seemed the last touch. He told me if I'd let him have my riding horse, he'd trade even for his section of land. And I did. He rode my horse off, and my wife and I, we stayed."

He looked out across the level, endless reaches of land.

"And today," he told me—although I think he was talking to himself more than to me—"today I'm harvesting thirty bushels of wheat to the acre from that section of land. Don't you think I did pretty good on the trade?"

My mind did some quick calculating. More than eighteen thousand bushels of wheat. For one horse.

"I think you did fine," I assured him.

"And," he added, as if it were important, too, "I've never done any of those things I promised the Lord I'd stop. I quit every last one of them, and stayed quit right up till now."

He had kept his promise, and the land had fulfilled every promise he had dreamed for it. Indeed, he had done well.

I thought about his story as I drove back to Amarillo. On both sides of the highway, far as eye could see, fields of wheat stretched out. Endless. Golden. Moving gently in the wind like the waves of the sea. I looked until I grew tired of looking and still there was nothing but distance. I felt myself growing small and even a little frightened, as a child is frightened in the dark for no real reason except it is a thing that encompasses him. "What is man that Thou art mindful of him?" the endless spaces seemed to ask.

Suddenly things began to come into focus. I remembered the preacher and his wish to write about "the special people who made this region." I remembered the stories the pioneers had recorded—how they withstood drouth and crop failures and prairie fires and loneliness. Ah, that was the hardest of all, the loneliness. Yet they had stayed on to make a region. It was the homesteader, not the rancher, whose story I wanted to tell. Without him there would have been no fields of wheat waving in the wind today; without him there would not have been an Amarillo, or at least it would have been, perhaps, nothing more than a small shipping point for the cattlemen. Unless they had come—all those people who settled the towns and built the roads and started the schools and churches—I myself would not be here. Now I knew what I wanted this book to be.

It would tell the homesteader's story. The nester—the little man who came out to farm a single section in a land where a section was a thing so small as to evoke the amused laughter of the cattlemen. It would be told with no wish to diminish the glory of the rancher, already so well established; rather I would draw attention to the fact that two groups of people built the Texas Panhandle. The rancher *and* the homesteader. Nobody as yet had written a novel about the homesteader and his place in this region. Here was my field. I had done what every writer must make himself do sooner or later: Reject the oft-told, the obvious, the preconceived notion that everyone holds as a matter of course. I suppose a writer just naturally needs to be a contrary person.

I went back to my material with a new sense of purpose. I talked with such pioneers as were still living and willing to talk.

A very old woman peered at me from bright, young-looking eyes, "Now don't you go making us the kind of women who ran screaming out into the wind, completely daffy," she admonished. "I've read a book or two about other places where pioneer women did just that. We may have wanted to, but we were always too busy. Besides, the woman that the wind could drive crazy didn't stay long enough for it to do the job."

In my reading I found instances of women who couldn't take it—the wind and the drouth and the loneliness. I put several of them into my book. I believe the ratio of those who stayed was one in four. By purest accident I hit that number right. From those who stayed there was one theme, oft-repeated: "That was our happy time," they all insisted.

They forgot the hardships and remembered only the final triumph. I was intrigued by their philosophy. They came out here, these homesteaders, knowing they were not headed for an easy life. They did not expect anyone to give them anything, guarantee them anything. They knew they had to pay for what they got, whether it was land or freedom or the good life, and the cheapest price they would pay was money.

The more I learned about these people, the more I liked them. Better than that, I respected them. For me, this is very necessary in any writing I do—that I feel respect for my characters. In no way does this mean I want them to be perfect, for I am a little frightened of perfect people. And suspicious. I have a great wish to dig in and find their weaknesses. A weakness on my part, perhaps, but a fact I have to face. It is necessary, however, that I believe in my characters and have sympathy for them, even in their weaknesses and their sinning. By and large, I tend to write about people I could ask in for a cup of coffee or a spot of tea.

I find it difficult to understand why authors create characters to whom, in real life, they would probably not give a second glance. The depraved. The degenerate, the weakling, the whining misfit. Is it a sort of twisted God-complex that makes it necessary to create something to which they can feel superior? Certainly I have no quarrel with the thesis that every writer has a right to select his own material, but as for me, I must like my characters. Not bow down in worship before them—just like them. I would not continue to wear out my two typing fingers conjuring up characters who, were they to walk into my room, would arouse in me the wish to push them out the door and air the room they had occupied.

My respect and admiration for these pioneers increased as I continued to read about them, talk with them or with their friends and descendants. I was increasingly determined to set them down accurately. Them, and the region they had settled. Later I found that in this latter endeavor I succeeded so well it would have been impossible to have moved the setting six months in time or three miles in distance and retained my story as I told it. The time element had something to do with a change in the law under which claims could be filed and was the result of careful research; the location was a happy accident, or maybe the reward for being a good girl and doing my homework.

By now, many people knew the nature of my project. Frequently someone would offer me a helpful piece of information.

One charming older woman, a rancher's widow, invited me to her house for lunch.

"I understand you're doing a book about Panhandle ranches," she said.

"No," I told her, "it's about a young bride who came to a homestead near Mobeetie in 1885. She was eighteen at the time."

"My dear," she said, her eyes shining, "I came to Mobeetie, a bride, in 1885. And I was eighteen years old."

It was almost as if my heroine had materialized before me, like a genie popping out of a bottle.

"Tell me," I begged. "What was it like? The country? Mobeetie?"

She told me about the town, the one which was at that time the metropolis of the Panhandle. I did not use the information in this book, however, but in a later one. The feel I kept, the realness of what she said.

I overheard two old men talking in a bank:

"John," one said, "did you know they're building out on that spot where we broke the wild horses?"

"Yes, I know," John answered.

They were not two old men in a shiny new bank. They were young again, standing in a wide open spot where neither banks nor towns were dreamed of. They were breaking a wild horse, scarcely less free than they themselves were.

I was no longer writing fiction. I was recording what happened to real people at a time so recent some of them were still discussing it. I redoubled my research efforts. Everything had to be exactly right. Almost it seemed the pioneers were looking over my shoulder, watching every word I wrote. I think I even fancied myself as the pioneer woman type. Facing the future with courage and imagination. Adaptable. Able to cope. As I read more about the sort of life these women led, I gave up my self-delusion. I realized what I looked like when I was too long away from a beauty shop and I could not face the prospect. The knowledge served to increase my admiration for these indomitable women.

A friend and her husband took me for a swing around the territory where the book was set. We checked terrain, judged distances, regarded both skyscapes and landscapes. We built a fire of cow chips so I would know the shape and texture as well as smell of them as they burned. Once we were back at their house, we spread out maps and did scale drawings.

Another friend called me to say excitedly that I must get in my car and drive north. There was a prairie fire in that direction. I drove. It was a very small fire, and I stayed back at a respectful distance, but I did see the licking flames and the rush of the wild things running for safety.

I studied a scale model of a dugout in the museum, checking it mentally for size against my remembrance of my grandmother's fruit cellar. I read and I read.

And I wrote.

As I had done with my other books (and as I still do) I wrote when and where I could. Sometimes it was a few pages; sometimes only a few lines. As always, at times I hated it, loathed it, wondered why I had ever started it in the first place. And, equally as always, I am sure at times it would be a perfectly awful book and nobody, absolutely nobody, would want to read it.

In a mood of great discouragement I wrote in my diary, "I haven't had a minute to write a word in almost three weeks. By the time I'm ninety, I'll probably have this thing finished."

One day in early November a former student dropped by my office to say hello.

"What are you working on now?" he asked.

"Something set in the Panhandle," I told him.

"Oh, so you've turned to the ranch motif," he said, as if he had known all along that's what I'd do in time.

"No," I told him. "It's about the homesteader. But he's giving me a hard time. He came here a little too early to homestead, but a little too late to start ranching."

"Looks to me as if he's sitting right smack dab on the edge of time," the young man told me.

When I answered, my words must have surprised him as much as they did me.

"You have just given me my title," I told him.

And so he had—*The Edge of Time*.

Maurice Crain, who had agreed to act as my agent, came to Canyon to visit his family at Thanksgiving time. Naturally he got in touch with me to see how the book was going. I handed him the portion of the manuscript I had finished, feeling full of righteousness. Hadn't I gathered material without end about this region, and wasn't I doing something nobody else had done? He would be pleased.

He read the manuscript, looked at me uncertainly. "What do you mean to do now?" he asked.

"Finish it, of course," I told him. What else *could* I do?

"I'll have it completed by the middle of March," I said. "Then I'll send it to you to pass on to Dodd, Mead. I am not teaching the second semester. I've planned a trip to Mexico with a cousin."

Which I had.

I don't remember exactly what he said to that. He went back to New York and I continued writing.

From that time on I seemed to have worked consistently. I also got the shots required for my Mexico trip. I found that a neighbor, wife of one of the professors, would type my manuscript. I was feeling full of virtue and accomplishment. I wrote in my diary early in January:

"Didn't sleep much last night. All keyed up over the book. Lay awake, selling it to a book club, *Saturday Evening Post* (as a serial) and the movies. Finally dropped off to sleep, and then back at work this morning, realizing how much needs to be done. The fizz is gone."

Even without benefit of fizz, I kept on working. Although I was not teaching, I was not without interruptions. People dropped by, and I was invited to various things I wanted to attend. I had agreed earlier to give a few talks. I was making preparations for the Mexican trip. Finally, on February 25, I wrote, "Off went the book manuscript. Hope it goes over. Never can be sure."

I was merely exhibiting becoming modesty. I was sure that before long I would be having letters from everyone at Dodd, Mead telling me what a wonderful piece of work I had done. Once the manuscript was on its way to New York, I took off blithely to San Antonio for a short trip with some teachers who were going to an English conference there. I was scheduled to give a talk. Besides, I had never seen the Alamo.

While I was gone, I decided to go by Brownwood and visit cousins, and by Austin and Dallas and look in on friends in both places. I came back to Amarillo late the evening of March 9 and spent the night at my sister's. The next morning, I went to Canyon—circling by the post office for my mail. Yes—there was a letter from Dodd, Mead. I took it home and sat down to read, feeling warm and happy inside because I knew pretty well what the contents would be.

My euphoria lasted for one short paragraph, the first, which contained the customary compliments. It ended with this sentence, "We think it is fundamentally such a good manuscript that we want to point out some ways in which we believe you can make it better."

The "ways" occupied six legal size pages, single-spaced. I read on, not wanting to believe what I saw. The criticism touched nearly every part of the book, and the essence of it was plain (or so I thought). The book simply didn't come off. The facts were accurate, yes. But the people—well, they weren't quite real. The letter bore Mr. Bond's signature, but I was sure it was a compilation of the opinions of various people in the firm.

Later my sister, who had read the manuscript before it went away, said, "I wasn't surprised. It sounded like a good Master's thesis. I expected to find footnotes at the bottom of every page."

That, of course, was the trouble, a problem which most writers of historical fiction must face. It is very necessary that we do much research. A certain glow comes over anyone digging into facts. After a while, these facts in themselves seem the real goal. In writing, we become in effect unconscious exhibitionists. We want to put everything we have learned into our story. "Look, look," we seem to say, "see what I learned. Bet you didn't know that!"

In the process, the facts crowd the characters into the background. The research remains real; the people become shadows, pushed about by the events.

Recently I have gone back and reread Mr. Bond's letter. I was amazed that he should take so much time to go into such minute details, not only concerning the weaknesses of the book, but ways in which to correct them. I was also convinced that he is probably one of the best editors any publishing house has been privileged to have. Down the years I have worked with him closely on practically every book I have written for Dodd, Mead. Generally his judgment has been right, his suggestions helpful and correct. But at the time I was reading his letter concerning the reactions to *The Edge of Time* I had no such generous thoughts. I was hurt down to the very depths of my being. My head ached, my heart ached, my self-esteem ached hardest of all.

My first reaction was: "I'll show them. I'll change publishers." Already, I had received a couple of polite nibbles from other firms. I am sure every writer gets them; there is nothing unprofessional involved. This was a good book; I could easily switch with it. My second reaction was to take advantage of Dodd, Mead's reluctant agreement, passed along in Mr. Bond's letter, to publish the book just as it was if I insisted.

I wrote two letters—both models for all letters that authors write in haste and hurt when their manuscripts fall short of what editors hope for.

To my agent I suggested that I change publishers, naming the two possibilities. To Mr. Bond I wrote a heated defense of my book, implying—well, I am afraid (although, unfortunately I did not keep a carbon) coming flat out and saying he just didn't know a good book when he saw one. This done, I went back and reread his letter.

We still laugh about this incident, he and I. Why one particular criticism should have set me off is more than I can say. Perhaps because it had the greatest ring of truth and, maybe, because it held a hint of ridicule. Of my cowboys he had said, "They (the cowboys) come galloping up out of the wings and onto the stage with the precision and the happy smiles of the chorus boys at the Roxy. They are coincidences on horseback."

That did it. Where I had been hurt, now I was mad. More than that, and better. I was determined. I'd show them. I'd rewrite that book, and they'd be sorry they had ever said a cross word about it. I did not bother to rewrite my hasty letter to him, but I did add a saving postscript. I said I was starting the revision and that in two weeks I'd be in New York, there to finish the job.

I mailed the two letters, the one to my agent, the other to Dodd, Mead. I also made a telephone call to my cousin in Kansas City, telling her the Mexico trip was off, explaining I must go to New York for conferences on the current book. Which, of course was truth. She said that was all right —she was sort of backing out about the trip herself.

The next day a letter came from Maurice Crain, having crossed mine in the mails. Essentially, he echoed Mr. Bond's comments, and even added a few original ones of his own. "If I were you," he advised, "I'd count ten before answering his letter."

Count ten! I hadn't even counted sub-zero, and my letter was in the mail now, past recalling. Seldom had I felt more alone, more inadequate, more helpless. I had promised to rewrite my book without knowing how I was going to do it, or whether my efforts would be in any way successful. I could see myself forever stuck on this one book, as I had known other writers to be. Dragging the manuscript from one writers' conference to another, attempting to enlist the aid of friends or critics, trying to make something out of a book which should be chucked into the nearest wastebasket and forgotten.

I wrote in my diary, "Reading. Trying to get hold of myself. Think I almost succeeded. What makes it so much harder is the fact that I was so sure they would like it. Oh, well—I never wanted to write this book in the first place."

Then I went to bed, sure I would not sleep a wink. That night, or maybe ever again. Lying there, I started a conversation with myself. It went something like this:

Myself: Feeling pretty sorry for yourself, aren't you?

Me: *I have every right to do so.*

Myself: Making a big production of the whole thing. You expect your students to take criticism, yet you curl up like a scorched leaf when it comes to you.

Me: *This isn't criticism. This is rejection.*

Myself: If you feel all that bad, why don't you give it up? There's no law that says you have to make yourself miserable just because your publisher didn't go into tailspins over your book.

Me: *But I said I'd rewrite it.*

Myself: Why don't you get busy then?

Me: *But I don't know how to start!*

Myself: Who are you to think you should know all the answers? All by yourself.

Well, who was I, anyway! I closed my eyes. *You know I*

can't do this by myself. I brought the words up from deep inside me. *I need help. I'm turning loose. Help me start in the morning.*

Then I dropped off to sleep. The next morning I began the revision of Chapter One. When it was finished, I mailed it. Then I started Chapter Two.

In the meanwhile, I had another letter from Mr. Bond, a short rather formal answer to the screaming one I had written him. It did little to soothe my hurt feelings, but I mailed him the revised version of the second chapter and started Chapter Three. Another letter came soon. Chapter One had arrived, he said, and it was good. Later I had some more details from Maurice Crain.

Mr. Bond had called him to say the first chapter had arrived and it was good. "She tells me she's sending more, but I doubt that it can come up to this."

"Why don't you tell her you like it," my agent suggested. "She's feeling pretty bad about now."

Mr. Bond's response to the suggestion was a telegram. It said, "First section much better. Hurrah. Second section just arrived. Letter follows."

The letter, when it came, was kind and helpful. And encouraging. I worked with more hope now. Two weeks from the day I had received the letter telling me the cold hard truth about my manuscript, I mailed off the last of the revisions I had planned to do before going to New York. A week later, I followed.

My arrival did not bear any aspects of a happy omen. The plane was delayed, so it was past midnight before we set down. I discovered my baggage had been left in Dallas. My hotel room, reserved ahead of time, was the sort allotted to transients whose status is not clearly defined in advance. I took a bath and crawled into bed, wearing my nylon slip and wondering why women thought a black nightgown was anything special.

The next day went better. My baggage came. Annie Laurie Williams, who knows New York the way she knows the palm of her hand, suggested that I move to another hotel, a small quiet, residential type. My room here proved ideal. I unpacked, feeling much at home as I did so. A call from Mr. Bond reaffirmed what he had already written—they liked the revision, and wanted me to come to the office for a conference the next day.

I came back from that conference with suggestions enough to help any writer do a dozen books. I rented a typewriter. And there in a New York hotel room, with the roar of Times Square in my ears, I rewrote my book. This time I was concerned with the people rather than with the historical facts, trying to capture them as they went about the various activities which were a part of their lives. Plowing up the prairie sod that had lain undisturbed since time began. "You could plow a straight furrow for two hundred miles with nothing to stop you," one man wrote in his memoirs. Planting their crops. Hauling water. Attending all-day preaching and dances. Fighting prairie fires and blizzards and drouth. The pioneer doctor came in as he made his rounds. So did the old preacher on his horse, Devil. And the woman who insisted on burying her baby back "where there were people." Of course, the cowboys were in it, too—knights of the prairie, mounted as had been their earlier prototypes, the Knights of the Age of Chivalry. Romanticized, of course, but not so greatly unlike the heroes legend has made of them.

But most of all, I wrote about Bethany Cameron, the little bride who had come to the Panhandle from Missouri and had known loneliness for a neighbor. Bethany who planted the rosebush beside their dugout and guarded it against drouth and blizzard and wind and animals, feeling instinctively that if it died, their dream died with it.

And, as was only right, I dedicated the book to the homesteader.

Maurice Crain, who had grown up in the Panhandle, helped me in the revision. Both he and Mr. Bond checked and rechecked and made suggestions. And when the gesture was indicated, they did not hesitate to beat my ears down. One day Mr. Bond telephoned to say a book club was interested, and could I bring the final pages of revision to the office at once. I said I wasn't finished yet, but he told me to bring the manuscript anyway. The club readers would understand. I went down at once, bearing the remaining pages.

Lilian Kastendike, who had done *The Years of the Locust* condensation for *Redbook,* called to say they were looking for a novelette. How about the one I was currently working on? I told her I questioned they would be interested, since this was a pioneer story. She said she'd like a look at the carbon anyway, if I had one. I took it to her, and then went back to my hotel room, strangely empty now with no manuscript to nudge me.

Patience is not one of my virtues. I shopped. I went to some plays. I did an autobiographical sketch requested by Dodd, Mead. This finished, I decided I couldn't stay in my room another minute without doing harm to the typewriter, the autobiography, or maybe even myself. I dressed and started down to Dodd, Mead, walking because I needed to work the kinks out of my disposition. When I went into the office, Mr. Howard Lewis, president of Dodd, Mead, and Mr. Bond were waiting for me.

"We were just trying to call you," they said.

I drew back, instinctively fearing bad news. Maybe they had decided that, after all, my revision wasn't so good. Maybe they wanted me to start all over again.

"How do you feel, Miss Loula Grace Book Club Erdman?" Mr. Lewis said, grinning at me.

"You mean. . . .?" My voice was the upward beat of a question.

"The Family Reading Club has taken it; Literary Guild has chosen it as an alternate selection. It's a Junior Guild recommendation."

I said, inelegantly, but with feeling, "Catch me, boys—I'm falling."

A day or two later, Lilian Kastendike called.

"Are you close to a chair?" she asked.

I happened to be sitting on my bed at the time, so I said yes.

"We're buying it," she told me. I didn't answer. "Did you hear?" she asked. "I told you we're buying it."

I said hollowly that I was glad. I don't know how convincing I sounded, but I am sure she understood.

By way of celebration I did two things. First, I called my family in Amarillo to relay the good news. Then I went out and bought a hat I had been coveting ever since I came to New York. Around the crown was a swirl of black fishnet type material to which were attached small pink forget-menots. "Handsewn," the saleswoman assured me, although I couldn't have cared less. The flowers were symbols of this book; I wanted to remember it always.

The next day I went back to Texas, much wiser than I had been when I arrived in New York. *The Years of the Locust* and *Lonely Passage* had both come too easy for my own good. In them I was merely retelling a way of life I knew well. A self-centered, self-contained report, akin to journalism. When I reached out beyond myself, as I had done in this book, testing new experiences, new ways, new knowledge, I understandably failed in my first attempt. Bitter as the experience had been in the beginning, I now could count it gain.

Perhaps it is good for a writer to experience frustration and heartache and despair and yes, even rejection. It gives sympathy and understanding and compassion not only to one's writing, but to all the other experiences of life. In writing, as well as in living, we need to have a restraining hand laid upon us occasionally. It is entirely possible that we learn more from our failures than from our successes. Certainly I had learned much in the rewriting of this book, and I think we are always glad for any new knowledge that comes to us, painful though it may be in the gaining. I question that Eve ever truly regretted having eaten the fruit.

Besides, you forget the hurt; in time you can bring yourself to laugh at it. Even so, it always stays with you, just a little. Like the fragrance that lives in the rose you once pressed. When you come across it, years later, you find it difficult to remember why you were moved to save it in the first place. Then, holding it in your hand, the occasion comes back to you, and there it is, fresh and vivid as when it first happened. The happiness and the hurt and all the rest of it. However, as the lyric says, "Without hurt, the heart is hollow."

And when did anything good ever come from a hollow heart.

Chapter Eight

Writing is a type of addiction. With a project finished, an author may have withdrawal symptoms. The remedy for this is traditional—a hair of the dog that bit you. My book out of the way, I turned to short stories.

The psychological effect of writing a short story is that, being short, it is therefore easy to write. It may be short but it is far from easy. A good short story requires effort and time and revising and reworking; and, like any other piece of writing, a certain amount of agonizing. The entire process was pretty well summed up by a woman who once helped my sister.

"That boy of mine," she said, shaking her head sadly, "he's sure giving me a hard time. I'm laying off to give him a good whipping."

"Why don't you?" my sister asked, more for conversation's sake than from any wish to have the answer.

"Won't do him a bit of good if I don't get myself worked up to it first, and I ain't had time to do that yet."

Certainly it is necessary for a writer to be "worked up," to be deeply involved, in order to write a short story, just as it is necessary in any other type of writing. I had no illusions about the difficulty inherent in writing a short story. I knew, also, from past experience that even revising one already written was not easy. But since I had some unsold ones in my files I brought them out and began reworking them. A few sold. Most of them came back and back and back. In some ways it was a repetition of my first years of writing—my mailbox often held those brown envelopes, self-addressed and stamped. There seems to be an innate streak of stubborness in a writer which makes him keep trying long after good sense and judgment would indicate it is time to give up on a piece of writing. Some things are not meant to sell, just as all seeds do not germinate or all plans meet with success. Finally, I had to admit the truth about those oft-rejected ones and tuck them away in the hopeless file. Sometimes I wonder if it is possible for a writer to emulate Lot's wife. Standing forever in one spot, looking backward at something which should have been forgotten long ago, unwilling or unable to face forward and go on. Perhaps one of the most profitable lessons we can learn is to turn loose a thing not worth holding to.

I continued to write what is termed the plotted story. To me, the unplotted story, the slice-of-life thing, all too often seems like a whirl around in a revolving door. In the end, you wind up exactly where you started. Nothing has happened, and you really haven't been anywhere. All you had was a lesson in frustration. I say this even as I admit that many excellent stories of this type have been written; I set my classes to studying some of the better examples. Perhaps

the difficulty is that some writers—especially the younger ones
—feel an unplotted story is an unplanned story. That they
have only to set down whatever runs through their minds
and they will automatically come up with a story. What
they all too often produce is the tiresome monologue of a
compulsive talker.

In defense of the slice-of-life story its champions frequently
say it has more validity than the plotted one because life
itself is not plotted. In this contention they are in error. Plot
is, in essence, cause and effect. That is the basis on which life
rests. The difficulty lies in that we often have to wait a long
time before we can see this truth demonstrated. Perhaps
therein lies the pull of a plotted story—that it does make
sense. The reader is, either consciously or unconsciously,
reaching out, searching for answers which life itself has
denied. Wanting to make sense, wanting to believe.

This search is not confined to literature alone. Even those
who know little about music are moved by the beauty of
Beethoven's Fifth Symphony. Note follows note with logic
and order. This quality, this certainty, we seek in life. Writing should have logic and order, also. Which does not mean
at all that a piece of writing should automatically have a
happy ending. That is contrary to life. But it should make
sense; it should have some sort of sequence of cause and
effect.

The so-called "slick" magazines—usually the women's magazines—have been the most frequent whipping boy in this
feud between the proponents of the plotted and the unplotted story. Those who downgrade these magazines either
forget or overlook entirely the fact that many of our best
writers have appeared in them. Hemingway. Katherine Anne

Porter. There is a long list of impressive names. Portions of a Steinbeck novel appeared in a woman's magazine shortly before he won the Nobel prize.

The word "popular," too, has fallen upon evil ways, implying a lack of quality in a piece of writing. What is wrong with having people want to read something an author has written? Dickens was extremely popular in his day. Shakespeare's plays were so doted on by the masses that the nobility hesitated to attend public performances lest their sensitive nostrils be offended by the odors of the common folk packed tightly together in the theatre.

I once sat in an informal gathering while a distinguished author, now dead, held forth at great length on his extreme dislike for a certain popular magazine with a wide circulation. We listened without daring to interrupt the great man. Finally he stopped his indictment and grinned at us.

"Perhaps," he said, "I dislike them so much because they've always returned everything I sent them."

I find his remark coming back to me now when I hear anyone level scathing criticism at any piece of writing. It was, in part, responsible for a practice I began in my classes and which to this day I still continue. Each semester I read to the class something I myself have written, proceeding on the theory that if I give criticism I should also be able to take it. I have never learned to present my offering with complete assurance. My voice, as I begin to read, is not quite steady and sometimes the hands holding the manuscript tremble a little. I have reason for my unease; the class members treat me exactly as they would anyone else, pointing out weaknesses as well as strengths, pulling no punches. Invariably, however, the criticism is of great help.

I remember especially the assistance given in a short story for which the class even furnished the title, "The Boy on the Back Seat." A woman's magazine bought it. Later it was picked up by several anthologies. It has resold in a number of foreign countries. New York public schools used it in an experimental reading booklet. A young man on the magazine was largely responsible for its being bought in the first place. When I expressed surprise that he liked it so much, he said it was because of its theme. "Almost every man who ever amounted to anything," he told me, "was at one time, figuratively speaking, a boy on the back seat."

Which points up the theme idea I stress so much in my classes. "The reason for writing the story," as I sometimes express it.

Once after I had gone to some lengths to explain this theme, or underlying idea, or reason for writing—call it what you will—a puzzled older woman raised a timid hand.

"My brother-in-law needed money very much indeed. He decided to write a short story. Was that what you mean by a reason for writing?"

I tried to answer her, remembering as I did so my own experience with writing confessions and the episode of the woman writer who was "for the underdog so long as it was financially profitable for her to take that position."

Perhaps the woman's question was not too far off after all. I personally believe, however, that any piece of writing based on a theme or style or content simply because it is the popular one at the moment is phony and hollow. Perhaps even a little ridiculous. Patterned after Eli Whitney's theory of interchangeable parts, these offerings do little more than shift ideas from story to story. Is violence selling? Quick, let

us tack some on at this spot. Or sex? Or Social Significance?
Or Civil Rights? Grab a piece and nail it here. Presto! Pretty
soon we will have something which will be sure to sell because that is what everyone is saying now.

Before long, the output begins to resemble the rows of
packaged goods on supermarket shelves, differing only in that
they are "economy," "giant economy," or "super-giant-family"
sizes. I either push my grocery cart with all speed past these
items or avoid the aisle altogether. It is possible that the
writer who choses the theme simply because it is the most
profitable route for him to take does more harm than good
to the cause he professes to espouse.

Besides, anything slanted exclusively toward a current
trend becomes dated, even obsolete, almost before the ink
is dry on the paper. Essentially this is journalism, and however good reporting may be, it is still dated. As a newspaper
friend of mine says of her work, "Today's writing becomes
tomorrow's garbage container."

This is not meant to downgrade journalism. In a way, I
envy newspaper people. They have learned to say what they
mean on the first go-round. I falter. I use echo words. My
initial versions do not always convey the meaning I hoped
to put across. There is a discipline in news writing which, if
properly learned, can help any writer.

Certainly no author can ignore the events, attitudes, problems, and the essential nature of human beings in the world
in which we live. A rule of thumb test I use consists, roughly,
of two parts. First, do I really believe what I am saying?
Second, will I be able to approach the idea from a point of
view different from that generally used?

I suppose it gets down to that thing called "slanting," much as I feel the word is misused.

My writing was broken short the summer after I had finished *The Edge of Time,* as my writing is so often interrupted, by other duties pressing in on me. This was the year our English department decided to sponsor a writers conference, and I was considered the logical one to take over.

The conference was successful. We continued to hold one each summer for some seven or eight years. Later, the chore of running it was turned over to others in the department. And a chore it is, and don't ever forget it.

I am of a divided mind about this matter of writers conferences. Generally speaking, there are two main types. First, there is the one which does little more than give the would-be writers a chance to look at and listen to editors, publishers, and successful writers. The other is a workshop course, conducted as a class would be. Both are attended by much the same sort of people hoping, perhaps by a process of osmosis, to pick up hints on writing, slanting, marketing, and all the other problems which have dogged writers since Caxton first hit upon the miracle of the printing press.

These conferences vary from ordinary to excellent. I personally favor the workshop type, perhaps because that was the sort we held on our campus. Ours lasted three weeks. The first one was filled with lectures and conferences by outstanding writers, editors, publishers, and agents. The last two weeks were given over to a workshop situation which I conducted. The class might be taken for college credit if the enrollee so desired. The first week offered information and inspiration; the others, a chance to work with the knowledge gained. Merely listening to someone talk about writing, no matter how brilliant or successful the speaker may be, is much like taking a swimming lesson in a gymnasium—you learn the theory, but there is no guarantee you will be able to swim once you are thrown into the water.

I have spoken at a number of writers conferences in various parts of the country. In my early writing days, I enrolled in one. (About all I remember is that Carl Sandburg spoke and I was much impressed with his poetic voice. I also recall he wore an open-necked shirt and neither coat nor tie and sang his own poems to the music of a guitar which he himself strummed.) As to the conferences where I have spoken—I always wonder if I gave anyone any real help, or at least enough to justify my being there.

From my experience in both camps of the writing conferences, I have come to the conclusion it is pretty well up to the one attending as to whether he gets any real help. If he comes expecting to find a magic key which will open all the doors in the writing world, he is letting himself in for a great disappointment. If he looks upon the experience as an opportunity to listen to—and perhaps meet and have a discussion with—successful authors and others in the writing field, he will be able to achieve his objectives. There is, also, a fringe benefit, one not to be dismissed lightly. Here is a chance to mingle with others who are struggling, as he is struggling, to break into the writing game or to improve the quality of what he is doing. Writing is essentially a lonely business. It is a paradox that we who are supposed to write

reluctant permission, I took it inside the living room. There, to my great feeling of triumph, I found I could manage one pretty well, thanks. I was going fine when one of the little girls peeped in the front door and saw me in action. She went back to my mother.

"Your grandmother's in there trying to play with my Hula-Hoop," she reported.

To me, the story is more than funny. It's an allegory of the best type for authors who aspire to write books for children. Any time we try to act kittenish, try to make the children think we are right down on their level—one of them, as it were—we wind up by looking like our own great-grand-mother. Best we write material for young people straight, the way we write for adults.

I found this new book easier to write than *The Edge of Time* had been. Of course there were the notes, the real-life incidents gained in my research, much of which had not been used in the earlier book. Also, the date was a later one, making it possible to talk with people who had either grown up during the period of which I proposed to write or whose parents had. There were anecdotes without end; there were escapades and events sufficient to fill half a dozen books. My problem was selection. Actually, everything I put into the book happened to some Panhandle family at some time. All except the episode of the little dog breaking up the prayer. That happened to the Erdman family, once upon a time.

But a juvenile is not easy to write, simply because it happens to be for young people. I alternated between thinking it was mildly awful and terrifically terrible. I have consulted my diary and find such entries as follow:

"Tonight I wrote the first few pages of the new book.

Those are almost invariably the ones I have to throw away, but even so, it's good to have something to throw away."

"Worked so hard and long, I feel like a piece of tired elastic. Writing for young people is not easy."

But there were bright spots. For one thing, I again had young people reading my manuscript, ones the approximate age of those I hoped my book would interest. My niece and one of her friends came to spend the weekend with me, knowing they were to read what I had written, feeling grown-up and responsible. Who knew but what the whole future of the book rested right on their shoulders! They sat cross-legged on my bed, passing typed sheets from one hand to another. I worked at my desk.

"Lou," Molly Lou told me (I had long since ceased to be "aunt"), "I don't like the title."

The working title at the time was a tentative one, something like *The Bright Sky,* as I recall.

"Off with its head," I promised.

They read on.

"Lou," Jane T. said, lifting big expressive eyes to my face, "I can just feel the *tense* of this."

I knew she did not use the word in a connotation of time, but, rather, to mean "tenseness." I accepted the real definition and cherish it to this day.

They continued reading. I turned my mind toward a new title. A memory came back to me. It was the first weekend in Texas for my sister and myself, and we were homesick. And, let's face it, somewhat appalled at the unending distances which apparently surrounded Amarillo. Mrs. Warner, who had been responsible for our coming, must have sensed how we would feel. She had asked us to come to the small town some thirty miles away, where she lived. We went by bus, the ride through those open windswept treeless spaces doing nothing to make us like the country any better.

Once at her house though, being fussed over and fed and made to feel welcome, we cheered up. Of course, she asked the conventional question, "How do you like the Panhandle?"

"It's all right," I hesitated, evading the question. And then I added, "If only the wind didn't blow so much."

Mrs. Warner looked at me keenly. "Don't fuss about the wind, Lou," she told me. "It has made it possible for our kind of people to stay here."

Later I was to understand the full implication of what she said. The wind, indeed, had helped the homesteader to stay on, for it furnished the power to turn the windmills which, in turn, furnished the water enabling the homesteader to take root. The little man, on his single section. It was free power; it was more than that. It was the spirit of the country. The cowboy ballad expressed the thought. "The wind blows free," it said.

"I have my title," I told the girls. "How does *The Wind Blows Free* sound to you?"

They said it was fine, just fine. And they began singing the ballad, a little off key.

Both those girls are women now, married and with children of their own. Both have the various copies of *The Wind Blows Free* in their libraries—first editions, the German, the English, the Arabic—the latter with its back to front, left to right, beautifully artistic script. I would like to think the book will be available when their own children reach the age to read it. Isn't that the great hope of all writers

—that their creations will go on and on in a kind of immortality? Why else do we write?

In doing *The Edge of Time* I had known the altogether satisfactory experience of having editors help me in the business of revision. It is one thing to sit at your typewriter several hundred miles away, groping for the right revisions and, once they are done, sending them off, only to wait days or even weeks before knowing the verdict. It is quite another situation to do the revising in a hotel room, grab a taxi or bus and rush down to the editor in minutes, there to have immediate reaction to what you have done. I had found revision-on-the-spot to be so satisfactory that I decided to try the same technique with this new book.

I sent off a fairly complete version of the manuscript to New York. In due season, I followed.

This time, I was working with Dorothy Bryan, that knowledgeable and capable juvenile editor at Dodd, Mead. I holed in at the same small, quiet hotel, rented a typewriter, and began work.

Immediately, Miss Bryan put her finger on some of the weaknesses. Katie, the younger sister, had run away with the book. (I am sure many writers have experienced that same difficulty. A minor character sometimes steals the show completely.)

"Push her into the background," Dorothy Bryan said. "You can use her in another book."

"Not me," I said. "Who do you think I am—Martha Finley, setting out to do a new *Elsie Dinsmore* series?"

(Dodd, Mead had been the original publishers of those famous books.)

She let that pass, but I am sure she knew, even then, that some day I would write the book she suggested.

Of course, Maurice Crain, with his inexhaustible knowledge of the Panhandle, gave much help when I faltered. Friends in Amarillo were on the alert to locate material that might be helpful. In fact, the first chapter had to be rewritten because someone there came across a small item which showed Amarillo to be a little different from the way I had pictured it at the time the Pierce family arrived.

The book was finished and ready to go to press when Dorothy Bryan suggested we enter it in the *American Girl*-Dodd, Mead contest. Since my relations had been most cordial with that magazine, and with Marjorie Vetter, the fiction editor, I was easily persuaded.

For use in the magazine, the *American Girl* wanted a condensation, which I myself was supposed to do. At the moment I felt that I never, never wanted to look at a typewriter again. Never, as long as I lived. I think I almost felt the same way about the book itself. Still, the revision had to be done. I dragged out the bedraggled original manuscript, which only some kind providence had prevented me from chucking into the wastebasket the evening before, thinking I no longer needed it with the book at the publisher, and looked at it with utter loathing. It was at that moment providence again took over. Marjorie Vetter called to say that if I wished, she had someone who would do the revision. Did I wish? Does a drowning man wish a life preserver!

That was how Muriel Fuller came in on the scene. She was herself a writer and an editor, with a wide knowledge of young people's books. She came to my hotel room; we had a conference, and she left with the manuscript. The revision she finally came up with was the finest one of its kind that I have ever seen. *The Wind Blows Free* won the award. The condensed version was serialized in the *American Girl*. The book itself was published in 1952. Almost immediately the letters began to pour in.

"*The Wind Blows Free* is the best book I ever read. Write me, please, right away and tell me if it is based on truth or is it just a story? Was there a real Melinda Pierce?"

"Carolyn reminds me of my baby sister. She meddles in my boy problems."

"From Germany I send you many loves. Tell me—are things as you say in Texas? I cannot believe it is really like that."

"A cousin in the States sent me your book, here in Wales, where I live. I think it is the best book I have ever read. Please write another one to follow it."

"You mention vinegar pie. Is there really such a thing? If so, how is it made?"

(I had shared her doubts about the vinegar pie, mentioned so often by the early settlers. I found a recipe and followed it to the letter. While I did not feel the finished product merited the acclaim it received, I was still able to send her the recipe together with the information that I myself had used it.)

"Please send me all the facts of your life. How old are you?"

"Thank you for sending me your picture. My Maltese cat got up to the bulletin board where I had it and chewed it up. Please, may I have another one?"

"I don't see why people say this is a girl's book. The brothers were the bravest and smartest ones in it. I am a boy twelve years old."

The letters continued to come; they still come. Those earlier ones almost invariably asked for more books about the Pierce family. Eventually, there were two more. *The Wide Horizon,* the second on the list, was dedicated to Dorothy Bryan, for it was Katie's book, which she had suggested I do. There was an added interest for me in this one. My niece, Elizabeth Ann Erdman, did the jacket design before she took off to Paris to spend a year at the Sorbonne studying art. Often young people say now, "That's the best jacket on any of your books. It shows young people the way we look to ourselves."

I continue to receive letters about these books.

I value these letters because they tell what children themselves think. They do not mirror the selections made by parents, grandparents or fond aunties who buy what they think children should read. Never are they excerpts from current reviews. Rather, they represent the children's views and children pull no punches.

I have grandnieces and nephews. Grandparents show pictures; I "just happen to have" anecdotes which I quote on various occasions. One which I think is particularly fitting about this matter of making selections has to do with young grandnephew Ives, aged six, and his sister, Thalia Dee, barely eighteen months old at the time.

A young playmate, no doubt influenced by the neighborhood custom, was having a garage sale featuring an assortment of toys. Ives came in to ask his father for money and, with coins in his hands, went forth to buy. He came back with what seemed, even to us, really good bargains.

"You see," he explained, "these were the ones I wanted."

He turned to his sister. "See," he said, "I picked them out myself."

Small as she was, she seemed to understand there was something special and different about these toys. They represented his own choice, his own discoveries. So it is, I think, with reading material. The most prized, the most valued, are the books children discover for themselves. We could all learn from their honest approach. They do not read a book because they think they should, or because they saw it lying on a friend's coffee table, or because, currently, it is the correct thing to do. Children speak the truth as they see it; they make no pretenses. About them there is a sort of folk wisdom, instinctive, uncorrupted. Rarely are they attracted to a book simply because it is labeled "children's" or "young people's."

I also have many letters from young readers about my adult books, just as adults write me about the ones which fall into the category of children's books. I choose to believe this helps to prove my theory concerning the advisability of slanting. Don't! Rather, write the best book you know how to write and hope someone will want to read it.

Chapter Nine

One of the questions frequently asked a writer is "How do you get your ideas for a book? Or a short story? Or an article?"

There are various ways. They may be, as was the case with *The Edge of Time*, suggested by someone else. They can be born as a result of some incident or something one reads or hears or sees. Some of them are easy to brush off; some are gadflies giving you no rest, buzzing around no matter how hard you may try to push them aside; some are like the seed of a slow growing tree—they lie dormant a long time and finally, nurtured by a force you cannot always understand, they burst into bloom and can no longer be ignored.

All of them have one thing in common, however. In their inception, they sound marvelously wonderful and never offer the least hint that they will give you any trouble in bringing them into a complete and satisfactory form.

Times without number, someone (usually a student, often

an amateur) will ask, "Now wouldn't such and such an idea be a good one for a book? Or a story? Or an article?"

I always say of course it would. Any idea has a potential. The test is how you go about writing it. And always I add my warning; don't talk about a project until you have a sizable portion written, and then discuss only what is already on paper. I am superstitious about this. I feel preliminary discussions are not only bad luck, but also take away the fizz, the spark. There is something about keeping an idea bottled up inside yourself that seems to give it added force.

One of the occupational handicaps a writer must face is the letters from people who are either writing a book or plan to write one. Sometimes they will enclose an outline or even a portion of the manuscript in progress. Some merely ask for your opinion. Some want criticism. Some ask if you would like to co-author the book.

Of course, no writer will let herself get involved in any such proposition. I usually can reply, in all truth, that I am presently working on a manuscript and have neither the time nor the wish to undertake anything else. I say, further, that my contract with the school specifically forbids my working with anyone not enrolled in my classes. There are some very sound reasons back of this ruling, but even if there were not, I am only too happy to comply with it. Occasionally people either cannot or will not take my answer as a final one. I recall at the time I was in New York to receive *The Years of the Locust* award, a man, obviously older, called my hotel and was most persistent in wanting to outline his idea. I stopped him in mid-sentence, telling him it was indeed an excellent one—too good, in fact, to turn over to anyone else. By all means, he himself must do the book and receive the full credit and benefit from it.

Usually these ideas, these suggestions for collaboration, are sent in writing. These I return immediately. I have been known to use special delivery registered mail, with a return receipt requested. I also keep a carbon copy of my reply, together with the envelope in which the material came to me—the date on it is a record. Any number of well-known authors have been—still are—accused of using someone else's material.

Of course, this does not mean that everyone who writes asking for help has sinister designs on an author. A great many sincere, honest writers ask for guidance. By now, I am pretty well able to recognize these and I try to suggest sources of available help. But write their books with them I will not.

Rare indeed is the book (or story) for which information does not exist. Each author makes his own variations of a theme, using material that is there for the taking. Even so, some people still have a field day accusing writers of picking other brains, quite forgetting or entirely overlooking the fact that ideas in themselves are only the starting point. It is the use to which they are put that makes the book.

The idea for my book, *The Far Journey,* came to me when I overheard a conversation about a woman who had driven in a covered wagon from Missouri to Texas in the early nineties with only her small children for company. The incident fascinated me. Stories of families going west are a dime a dozen; a woman alone, or with small children, who would be more a liability than a help, was another thing again. I tucked the memory of the incident away in a corner of my mind, thinking that I would look for additional information about the trip and, perhaps, some day turn it into a short story. Incidentally, I never did gather any additional material beyond the conversation I heard by chance.

That summer, my mother and I drove to Missouri to visit friends and relatives. As always, the time was given over to much talking and laughing and to eating the delicious meals prepared by aunts and cousins and others. Then it was over and we were headed for Texas. Some friends who had recently made the trip suggested a route new to me.

"Not much traffic," they said. "Good roads."

They failed to tell me there was little traffic because the route went through territory practically uninhabited. Of course they had no way of knowing the thermometer would go into the upper nineties the day we made the trip. And perhaps it seemed of no importance that my car was not air-conditioned and that, since my mother did not drive, it would all be left to me.

To this day, I do not know the name or number of the highway we traveled. I sometimes suspect, in the light of what we came through, that my well-meaning friends took the map and, after eliminating all known roads, finally worked out a route for us to follow. The towns were far between; the towns were small; the towns were nonexistent. Mile after mile of vacant prairie stretched out on both sides of the highway. Sometimes in the distance we saw houses, small and forsaken looking. I felt much like the poem about Columbus. "Not even God would know, if I and all my men fall dead."

Mama was an excellent traveler. She wore a hat and white gloves, as befitted a lady who was taking a trip. She sat beside me quietly, making no complaint. So when she said, in the middle of nowhere in the middle of that blistering hot afternoon, "I wish I had a drink of water—and maybe an ice cream cone—" I knew she was expressing real need.

"The next place we come to we'll stop," I promised.

It was almost an hour before we came to "the next place," a filling station. We sat in the shade of the small building— really a shack—while we ate ice cream and drank our tepid sodas. (I suspected the water. I almost hesitated to allow the attendant to put it into the car.)

Then we started off again.

"The next place" was even more distant this time. I began to wonder if, by any chance, I had taken a wrong turn after we left the filling station. No, that was impossible. There hadn't been any, except ones into narrow gutted field roads. Maybe the highway had run out. Maybe it had grown tired of never being used and had given up being a highway.

"Mama," I said, "did you see a sign telling us what this highway number is?"

"Yes, honey," she told me with the conscious pride of a child who has come up with a necessary piece of information, "It's two numbers—fifty-five at night and sixty in the daytime."

I couldn't let myself smile, much less tell her the nature of her mistake—that she had given me the speed limits. Besides, I was too busy with my own thoughts. Clear as anything the way was straight before me. That woman-driving-through-alone incident was not a short story. It was a book. My mother's naïve reply had opened up a whole new train of thought. I was so busy pursuing the idea I gave scant heed to the heat and the discomfort and the dust. We reached

Amarillo in due season, and, after stopping for a bite to eat and some visiting with my sister and family, we drove on to Canyon.

The idea for this book would not leave me. A woman driving through with only a child for company. She would be responsible, as I had been in the trip just finished. She would not want to communicate her fear, as I had refrained from doing, lest my mother be disturbed. Mama had trusted me to do the right things; a child would have trusted. But, also, she had felt concern for my comfort, a wish to help. That, also, would be a child's reaction.

Fortunately, we lived next door to a family with a five-year-old boy. There was my model, my guide. I could watch him, talk with him, check his reactions. (Later one of the reviews said, "And in the book you'll find one of the most endearing little five-year-old boys in all literature.")

I was not a stranger to fear on a trip, either. Real fear, at night. Not imagined, but something for which there was a reason. It happened soon after I had bought my first car. I had talked in a Panhandle town some one hundred miles to the north of Amarillo. I had meant to start home early, in time to reach Canyon well before dark, but I delayed to have dinner with some former students, so by the time I got on my way it was later than I had realized. I told myself I was not afraid, with scant success. Actually, I am not a very brave person. I locked my doors, checked my gas, and took off.

Then, with no warning, the car stopped. I jiggled all the gadgets in sight and nothing happened. Absolutely nothing. I looked around me. I was in the outskirts of a town. This was, obviously, a—well, in the phraseology we would use today—this part of town was badly in need of urban renewal.

A small cafe sign across the street drew my attention. Lights—that would mean a phone. I would telephone a garage. I had barely laid hand upon the door when a man's figure materialized out of the darkness.

"Lady," he said, and even with the first syllable I knew he was more than a little drunk, "Lady, you are in a very bad part of town."

As if I hadn't already suspected that.

"Don't trust any of these people. Don't get out of your car."

People were surrounding my car now, with the air of wild creatures creeping out of the woods to see this strange thing which had happened to come into their midst. Black faces, white faces, all the shades between. They didn't say anything —they just looked at me and at the man standing beside my car.

"I'll call the garage for you," he told me, and moved unsteadily away in the opposite direction from the cafe and the phone I had felt sure would be there.

A young Negro boy pushed past him. The man ripped out an oath.

"Shaddup," the boy said. Then he turned to me. "Know any garage people in town?" he asked.

"Yes," I said, and named them.

"You just sit right there in your car," he told me. "Hear me? You aren't to get out. Maybe you'd better lock the door. I'll call the garage."

He was gone, briefly. When he came back, he said, "They'll be here in a minute." Then he stepped aside. Not out of sight, just standing between me and the man who had first appointed himself as my protector. There was a brief verbal encounter between them. But before real trouble, if indeed it was indicated, broke out, the garagemen arrived.

They towed my car to the garage and there began the usual tinkering and all those mysterious motions repairmen make over faltering machinery. I sat inside the office and waited. By and by they came to tell me all was well; I could go on now with no difficulty. I paid them and got into the driver's seat. The young mechanic followed me.

"You going to Canyon?" he asked.

"Yes," I told him.

"If I was you," he said, "I wouldn't take the cutoff. That's where *he* lives." He made a gesture, and sure enough, I saw the man who had first approached my car. The one who had warned me about the people of the locale in which I was stalled. He sat in a car, an old one it was true, but still a car, and he was watching me through the window.

"I'll sort of keep an eye on him until you have a good start," the mechanic told me. "But I'd take the long way home if I was in your place."

The obviously sensible thing for me to have done, in the face of such a warning, was to have spent the night at a good motel in this town where I had been stalled. Instead, I started back to Canyon, taking the "long way."

Just before I reached Amarillo, I was conscious of a car following me. Oh well, I thought, it will go on its way, once I come to Amarillo. It didn't. When I turned on the road to Canyon, it was right behind me.

I drove fast. It speeded up, maintaining the same distance between us. I drove faster. It increased its pace. There was but one conclusion. The car was following me.

I began to sing at the top of my voice, "His Eye Is on the Sparrow." Then it occurred to me that a car wouldn't trail a sparrow, and I giggled, only to catch myself with the guilty air of one who, in the face of great danger, has just committed a mild form of blasphemy. I sang louder, pressing my foot harder on the gas. And so, at last, I came to my house.

I stopped. The car was behind me; it stopped, too. By now I was no longer singing. I sat still a minute, considering the situation. It was only a few steps to the door, and the neighbors' houses were very close, and I had a good pair of lungs. Still, much could happen in those few steps from car to door, and young people sleep soundly. I fingered my door key. Sometimes it did not work too well. I had not left the stoop light on, thinking that I would be home long before dark.

For one wild, impractical moment I considered sitting there in my car the rest of the night. After all, it was locked. Then, I knew I would do no such thing. I opened the car door, started toward the house. The man in the car also alighted. I could hear his steps following me, sounding loud as doom, holding the ring of all the fearful dangers that ever befell a woman alone at midnight in a deserted place. I stood before my own door, prepared for anything. On one count I was determined. The man was going to have a good fight on his hands. I turned to face him as he stood directly behind me.

And I saw a highway patrolman.

"Lady," he said, his voice awed and a little shaken, "do you have any idea how fast you were driving?"

He stood there, pencil poised over pad, acting as if he did not in the least believe the figures he must record.

"Officer," I said. I am sure it was relief which made me answer as I did. Relief, and the sudden reaction from fright to a feeling of safety. "Officer—have you any idea of how scared I was?"

Without another word from either of us, I unlocked the door and walked inside, closing the door in the officer's face.

I never heard another word from the patrolman. No ticket for speeding, no warning, no anything. But because of him, I did know what it meant to feel fright in the dead of night— alone, with a threat of danger and only myself to meet it. It was a knowledge which would serve me well in the writing of the book.

I had other assets in my favor—the inexhaustible riches in our museum and the help given me by its curator, Boone McClure, who was thoroughly familiar with both the history and geography of the region. He drew a rough map for me.

"This is the road she would have traveled at that time," he said.

He put in small circles at intervals.

"These represent the probable camp sites," he continued.

He went into details concerning the character of each place where my heroine stopped and some of the things that could have happened to her there.

Some of these possibilities posed real threats to her safety. No light undertaking, this journey. She must have a true and definite reason for making it alone.

All right, I asked myself, why was she alone?

As far as that went, why did she start in the first place?

Writing is a constant succession of "why's" which the author must put into the mind of the reader and then, if possible, answer them. Recently I overheard my six-year-old grandnephew and my three-year-old grandniece in earnest conversation. He was telling her about a television show he had seen. Ever so often he would stop dramatically.

"Know what?" Allan would ask.

"What?" Robin would demand, leaning forward eagerly.

Then he would continue with his recital.

Good writing is like that. The author spins the yarn, injecting enough suspense to hold the reader's interest; in effect, asking "Know what?" And the reader, with interest aroused, continues to ask "What?"

At intervals Robin would respond, after Allan had given more of the incident, "Oh, that was good." Once her response was evidently not the correct one.

"No," he told her, "it was bad. Very bad indeed. You weren't listening."

It would be most convenient for writers if we could always blame our readers when the meaning of a story does not come through. This we cannot in good conscience do. We must assume the fault was ours and set about making our meaning so clear that there will be no confusion in the mind of the reader.

I found a reason for my heroine's traveling alone. The pieces began to fall into place. "Know what?" traveling the route she took, she would probably meet an outlaw of some sort. "Know what?" she must have a gun. But she had never handled a gun. Neither had I. So, I decided to check for myself how a woman firing a gun for the first time would feel.

In order to test my reactions I went to a shooting gallery just off the campus. I had absolutely no success in handling the gun provided me. About all I accomplished was to frighten the living daylights out of the young attendant.

Looking at him I had the answer. My heroine, Catherine Montgomery, would never hit an outlaw; she must do something else, something that would frighten him or infuriate him as much as would a bullet singing in his direction.

Some of my difficulties came from New York. An editor there, one who had some knowledge of the setting of the book, protested that Catherine could not have followed the route I had her travel, since there was no road there at the time of my story. A friend of mine found an old map in a secondhand bookstore in Oklahoma. On it the road was marked, plain as could be. I promptly sent it to Dodd, Mead.

There came another objection from the same editor. He contended the flash flood my heroine encountered as she crossed the Canadian River was not possible at that particular spot.

I had the letter—let us say on Tuesday. On Wednesday morning, headlines in the Amarillo paper told of a flash flood which had occurred the day before at the same spot where I had placed the one in my book. Without comment, I sent the story to Mr. Bond. His reply was not long in coming.

"By now," he said, "we should know better than to question any of your research. Each time we do, the Lord himself steps in to vindicate you."

Of course he was joking, but even so, there was an element of truth in his comment. I go to great lengths in order to make my research careful and intensive, my facts accurate.

The Far Journey, inspired by a chance remark I overheard, started out to be a short story and grew into a book. As such, it has itself traveled far. It was a book club selection in this country. It was serialized in the Kansas City *Star*.

I held the first installment in my hands and was taken back across the years. Once more I sat with the family on a winter evening (we did not follow the custom in summer) while Mama and Dad, occasionally letting me have a short try, since I was the oldest child, took turns reading the current serial aloud. Two installments we got each day, the morning *Times* and the afternoon *Star*. Usually the portion given us ended with some sort of cliff-hanger, so we could scarcely wait for the next day's papers. Later, when we outgrew these reading aloud sessions, we all continued to read the serial on our own. It came back to me now, seeing my own story as a *Star* serial—the wonder, the delight, the suspense I had once known. Even if nothing else in the way of recognition had come to *The Far Journey*, I would have felt rewarded. But more did come. It went to England and to Germany. It was distributed by a book club in Holland. I have had letters about it from many people in many places widely scattered all over the world. One of the most interesting incidents came recently when I was in South America. A woman from Holland said, "Erdman—Erdman—someway that name is very familiar to me. How should I know it?"

She continued to question me until finally I suggested that perhaps she had read the book in her country.

"Of course," she said. "That's it. I remember that book."

She proceeded to prove her statement by telling me something about it.

A very far journey indeed—from Missouri to Mobeetie and then to Holland and back to a dinner table in South America. I think the woman who made the original journey, the one that set me to writing the book, would have been pleased.

The idea for *Three at the Wedding* came, obviously enough, at a wedding. To this day I do not understand why

I was invited. I knew the bride not at all, the groom and his family only slightly. Not only were most of the guests strangers to me, they seemed to be strangers to each other. At the reception, small groups stood about, obviously ill at ease, as I was. The sensible thing to have done was to join some of them. Instead, I stood by myself, making up stories about them and the principals in the wedding. The young woman who looked so unhappy—was she, perhaps, in love with the groom? The couple so obviously out of place. Poor relations? Divorced father of the bride? The possibilities were endless. I found myself weaving a plot about them, these people who were in all likelihood no more involved with the wedding party than I myself was. I began to have a very good time indeed and stayed longer than I had intended. When I left, I had an idea for what I thought would be a short story.

For its central character, I would have the unhappy-looking young woman who was attending the wedding of her lover to another girl. But the father of the bride (my imagined one) kept coming in. The woman with him was obviously his second wife. And the mother of the bride—how would she feel? I had no choice but to weave them all in. Before long, the story got out of hand. I was at the ready-to-throw-it-out stage when a young former student came down to spend the weekend with me.

"What are you working on?" she asked.

"This." I pushed the pages toward her. "Read it quick—I'm just ready to burn it."

She read. When she had finished, she said, "Lou, you have something here. Keep at it. I am already involved with these

people, and want to know what will happen to them. It's
a book, of course."

"No," I told her. "I meant it for a short story. But, as you
see, it's already much too long. . . ."

"A book," she insisted.

"No," I protested. "The idea is too slight for a book. . . ."

"I wouldn't be so sure," she said.

"As of now, I am," I insisted, and then we went on to talk
of other things.

Not long after that I had a letter from Lilian Kastendike
of *Redbook*. "By any chance," she asked, "do you have a
book in the works?"

Then it came to me that I might be able to turn this
oversized short story into a novelette which would find favor
in Lilian's eyes. I began working again. The project had
caught me up and I was running with it. Working hard and
long. Writing, rewriting. Discarding. By and by it was finished, and I sent it to my agent, calling it what I thought
it to be, a novelette. His reply was quick and definite.

"You have a book here," he said. "Write it."

I began expanding the material into a book. The same
old routine of working and reworking and expanding scenes
I had cut short for a novelette. Adding new scenes, new
characters. Filling out those already in, putting flesh on their
bones. Weeks later I had what I thought was a book finished
and off it went. My agent turned it over to Dodd, Mead. I
went to New York in a few weeks, there to begin conferences.
This time, Lilian Kastendike was also working with me on
the theory that a condensed version might be possible for
Redbook.

I agonized; I vowed I couldn't do it; I went back to my typewriter and wrote another scene.

A young woman from Dodd, Mead read my manuscript.

"I think you should do this or that," she suggested hesitantly.

I would consider her idea and, in all probability, use it or at least in a modified form. One day she and Mr. Bond and Maurice Crain and I were having lunch together. Everyone was throwing suggestions at me, some of them quite contradictory to anything anyone else was saying.

"I can't get over it," the young woman marveled. "The way you take suggestions. . . ."

"Don't let her fool you," Mr. Bond warned. "She sits there saying, 'Yes, I think you are right.' and 'Yes, I can see you have a point.' And all the time she means to go back to Texas and do exactly as she pleases."

Actually it wasn't quite the way he said. I did take suggestions, with gratitude and, I feel, profit. I did study them. But in the last analysis, the writing of a book is the author's job. In a way, it's like a woman bearing a child. She may have sympathy and understanding and help, but she herself is the one who must bring that baby into the world. Only so far can criticism or help be given you. Sometimes the divergent opinions and suggestions may even do more harm than good, especially if given by those who are unqualified to pass judgment.

I continued working on the manuscript in New York. I went back to Texas, and like the girl in the song, "washed the back of my neck and brushed my hair and started all over again." Eventually I wound up by doing a novelette version, rewriting it into a book and condensing the book back into novelette form. *Redbook* did, indeed, publish it. Dodd, Mead brought it out as a book. Later, it was picked up by paperbacks. Even now, I still think it was one of the best books I have done—that it went more deeply into the minds and hearts of my characters than I have ever done before or since. After I had turned the manuscript over to Dodd, Mead, I left for Europe in March 1953.

I sailed on the *Andrea Doria*. Not on that ill-fated final voyage, but on an earlier, uneventful one. It was on board the ship that I had the idea for another book, one which could scarcely have been more alien to an ocean voyage on an Italian liner. At the time, it had no title; it was not written for several years. But the first notes, the germ of it, were scribbled down hastily on *Andrea Doria* stationery.

I was sitting on the deck talking with a small group which made up one of those informal associations one falls into on shipboard, thinking the relationship will be of a lifelong duration and finding it difficult in six months to remember the people's names.

"The first fifteen years of this century," an older man was saying, "That was the golden age. A man knew what he could depend on. For himself, and for his family."

The others began to voice their own opinions, some agreeing, some dissenting. I listened, only half interested, having no conviction either way. Then it dawned on me that they were discussing the period 1900–1915, a time which was marked by the beginning of World War I in Europe. A good time, indeed! What was his definition of a good time?

"Maybe," I ventured, "it seemed good because our country was so completely unaware of what was going on beyond our own boundaries."

That set off another round of discussion. Even as we talked, the deck boys came by, passing out a ship news sheet. One item caught all our eyes. Queen Mary, that grand old lady of England, had died. The other, a smaller item, dealt with some news of Russia, having to do with changes being made since the death of Stalin.

And I thought—here we had been sailing along, isolated from the real world. Occupied only with our own affairs such as the comfort and the service of the ship, the food, the activities provided for our entertainment, the people we met. Our own private world. Outside of this small orbit, another world was moving on, without our knowing, without our caring. The old Queen had been a part of the era our friend had been lauding, one of the most famous. And that other item, the one about Russia. Surely it could presage a new era in that country. These things had happened while we were completely unaware of what went on. It was, in a way, a duplication of the Golden Age the man had mentioned. I slipped off to my stateroom and, once there, jotted down a few notes which were, later, to be the starting point for *The Short Summer*.

When I did go back to them several years later one thought filled my mind. What was our country like in that summer of 1914 before the world went mad? Specifically, my own home region, western Missouri? I tried to search out as best I could the answer to my question.

First I talked with people old enough to have definite ideas about the period.

"Let me see," they would say, obviously trying to remember. "Oh, yes. . . ."

Then they would relate some remembered event or incident.

Later I was to discover they really recalled 1917, the summer war came to the United States. They did not remember 1914 at all.

I decided I would go to Kansas City in order to have a look at the files of the Kansas City *Star* and *Times*. My friends on the paper were of the greatest assistance. The back issues were on film; each day I found these films already set up for me when I arrived. I read every issue of the paper, morning, evening, Sunday from June 1, 1914, through September 1 of that same year.

It was an undertaking which confirmed my own suspicions. By and large, the people in Missouri did not realize the possible consequences of the situation in Europe. The *Star*, known as one of the greatest papers in the country, did not give front-page space to the Archduke's assassination. This was occupied, rather, by a story voicing fear that the Prince of Wales might turn into a sissy and, also, by another story giving the details of a murder scandal in Paris, one in which prominent people figured.

I read on. I knew what people were wearing that summer; the songs they sang; the shows they saw; the recipes women followed. I knew, also, the news they read every day when they opened their papers. By and large, though, few people seemed to think the trouble in Europe would touch them.

I tried to capture these people as they went about their daily lives. Attending the Chautauqua, where they were told about the shooting of Archduke Francis Ferdinand, heir apparent to the Hapsburg throne, and his wife in a town named Sarajevo, a place none of them had ever heard about before. Going to the annual band concert in the park which, by great fortune, happened to be on the same day as the opening of the Panama Canal, a coincidence nobody had foreseen when the date was set earlier in the year. The young people at a party where, to the great disapproval of the minister and various older ladies, they danced that new abomination described in the Kansas City *Star,* the Turkey Trot. The older people, delighted that the war in Europe had made the price of wheat go up but very unhappy with a recent abomination to come out of Washington, the federal income tax law.

That was the theme of *The Short Summer*—the unawareness of most of the people and the gradual awakening of some of them to the implications inherent in World War I in Europe. The title came from Samuel Johnson's "Winter. An Ode."

> Catch then, Oh catch, the transient hour;
> Improve each moment as it flies!
> Life's a short summer, man a flower;
> He dies—alas! how soon he dies!

The summer was, indeed, short. It was also without end, for its sequel is still begin played out on the world's stage. Men did die—they continue to die—because of some of the things that happened then. A way of life died with the passing of that summer and an age and patterns of thought and action.

As I said in my foreword, "After its days were over, nothing would ever be the same again."

Chapter Ten

Another question frequently asked (or, failing the asking, implied) a writer is, "Why do you write?"

Why indeed! Why do people climb mountains, or set out on expeditions to the utmost ends of the earth, or attempt to cross the ocean in a small raft? Why do they teach school or sell real estate or run for office? Who knows all the complex and various reasons back of any human endeavor? One of the best answers I have ever heard to this writing question was given by my young doctor-nephew.

At the time, he was at McGill University in Montreal doing his specialization in radiology, and had come down for a weekend in New York where I was in the process of discussing a manuscript with my publishers. He and a friend were having lunch with me. The young man, meeting me for the first time, was regarding me curiously, apparently not quite sure of my status. Was I a writer or a college teacher or just a generous aunt who meant to pick up the check? Finally he cleared his throat.

"... er ... ah, how did you get started writing?" he asked. The manner of his asking prompted my response.

"You want to write, don't you," I said, making it a statement, not a question.

He drew back in instinctive denial, as if I had just accused him of attempting to push his grandmother downstairs. Which of course made me all the more sure my assumption had been correct. Dr. Bob threw himself into the awkward moment in his best bedside manner.

"Of course he would," he said. "That is the great wish of every human heart—the wish to communicate."

Perhaps not only the great wish but the great need as well. Of individuals, of groups, of nations. And, in some not too distant decade, it may be the wish of planets as well.

A lot of nonsense has been peddled about writing, often by the very ones who should know better. It is both an art and a craft; it is a creative process and it is hard, grubby work. It is a thing of the spirit; it is at the same time a most exacting kind of discipline. In short, it is an endeavor calculated to separate the men from the boys, the doers from the dreamers.

It should not be (or so I feel) the outburst of someone who, feeling sorry for himself, asks his reader to join in his great wail. Writing is not a retreat into some private grief or personal deprivation. Nor is it legitimately a wallow in despair. An unhappy childhood or adolescence does not automatically produce a candidate for the hero of a novel. Hitler had an unhappy childhood; he murdered millions of innocent people and started a world holocaust. Dickens had an unhappy childhood; he gave the world *David Copperfield, Oliver Twist,* and *A Christmas Carol.* A vast difference exists between brooding over a personal deprivation or affront and the attempt to call attention to a universal injustice.

There is another angle to the situation, one voiced by the Virginian in Owen Wister's book of that name. The young schoolteacher, in an attempt to introduce the Virginian to culture, has read Browning's "Incident of the French Camp" to him. At the conclusion of the poem, Napoleon, realizing the boy's condition, says, "You're wounded!" Whereupon the boy replies, "Nay, I'm killed, Sire!" and (according to Browning) "Smiling . . . fell dead."

The teacher, disappointed to find the cowboy did not approve of the poem, demanded to know why.

"Now a man who was man enough to act like that," the Virginian explained, "would fall dead without mentioning it."

He had a valid point. People who are deeply hurt rarely are articulate about the nature and depth of the wound, often denying, even to themselves, the real truth. Sadness without a valid reason for its existence is a mark of youth. If and when people grow up, they cease to be enamoured with grief in the abstract. They have quite enough in life, thank you.

The obsession with grief and despair and evil is, possibly, a tacit admission that these experiences constitute a part of the adult portion of life. In essence, this is the meaning back of the eviction from the Garden. One of the Serpent's talking points was that, by eating, Eve would be as the Gods, knowing not only good (which was now her sole portion) but evil as well. She learned all right, but there is no record of her having discussed the flavor of the fruit, once she had eaten. Now that she knew both good and evil existed, she must have realized that life was made up of a contest between the two forces. There was nothing especially noble about the eating. But the struggle that came afterwards—therein lay the glory and meaning of life.

Roughly speaking, most people go through three stages in their emotional development and, consequently, in their attitude toward life. In their early innocent days when they are surrounded by love and protection, they are inclined to look upon the world, together with the people in it, as an extension of this goodness. Then comes the inevitable day when they discover the great and sinister force of evil. To some this proves a more shattering experience than it does to others. For a time the discovery leads to the conclusion that the world consists of only evil.

If, however, one matures and comes to know life as a total experience, he will go on to a third stage of his development. He will see that, while there is indeed great evil in the world, there is also good. Much good. To deny its presence is to be unrealistic. Scientists, doctors, philanthropists, to say nothing of ordinary people, are living their lives out as best they know how with only occasional lapses.

Personally, these are the people I know best. Women taking bowls of hot soup to neighbors, standing by when there is sorrow or trouble in the house; driving kids to school and dental appointments; getting meals on the table; mending cuts and broken hearts. Men going to the office and pretty well sticking to business all day; giving time to community activities or taking the kids on picnics; coming home to the Little Woman and the family at day's end. In short, behaving like adults, not arrested adolescents.

Strange then that the term "adult theme," should so often

be linked with violence, sex aberration, sadism, lawlessness, or some other type of behavior deviating from what is commonly accepted as the norm. Certainly as a former junior high school teacher I cannot see these themes as adult, especially the four-letter-word syndrome.

It is difficult for me to understand why this magic number should have come to have such evil connotation. There are all sorts of lovely words with four letters, such as *love* and *food* and *hope* and, yes, *book*. Besides, there are any number of words with five or more letters which do not exactly breathe out sweetness and light. But even when these four letter words are used in their usual sense (a designation which by now has become almost a cliché) I cannot accept them as adult but, rather, what I believe them to be—manifestations of adolescents who have just discovered sex and who, like the cavemen, are moved to record their newly acquired knowledge on basement walls. In junior high, the janitor used to report the matter to me, and I, in my role of freshman counselor, would name a committee of boys who, in turn, would see that the writing was scrubbed off. We teachers all regretted the incident, but said it was a phase the boys would outgrow. Grown men do not go about writing words on walls.

We took a similar attitude toward many of the other activities in which the boys (and sometimes, even the girls, although their record was considerably lower) engaged, ones now termed "adult." We tried to take appropriate action, comforting ourselves the while with the thought that by and by these adolescents would outgrow their present behavior.

Anyway it is not necessary to spell out an adult theme for a true adult. He will know what you are talking about and become bored with repetitious details. As a reader, he brings almost as much to his reading as he gets from it, maybe more. That is why French novels used to be considered so naughty —they used asterisks, giving to the reader the privilege of filling in the details. The truly knowledgeable person could run ahead of anything the author might tell him; the uninitiated would not understand if he saw a diagram. One of the most suggestive songs ever written is said to be "Colonel Bogie's March," theme song of the movie, *The Bridge on the River Kwai*. It has no words at all—everyone fills in from his own imagination.

Not only have I had too many of those magic-number words, I am also fed up with plays and books and TV programs which celebrate crime and violence and abnormalities. Reading them, seeing them, is almost like putting a coin in a slot at the automat—you know ahead of time exactly what you'll get once the door props open. More often than not the offering has been highly praised by critics and/or reviewers, rated the best of its kind.

What is "best" anyway? And who establishes the criteria for judging? And, once the verdict is pronounced, must I necessarily accept it, even if the one who gives it is a recognized authority in his field? Especially if I do not agree. There is no law which rules that people, like sheep, must follow a leader over a cliff.

Often after seeing or reading one of these offerings, I recall the remark of a woman I once met between acts at a Broadway play. It was both violent and disturbing and, I felt, a highly unrealistic picture of the segment of society it was supposed to represent. Even so, it had received the highest critical acclaim and some of the most coveted honors.

The woman and I were drawn together by a circumstance calculated to make any women notice each other. We wore identical costumes. After we had eyed each other silently for a few moments, I made my way to her.

"Would you mind telling me where you got your suit?" I asked.

"Melbourne, Australia," she told me. "Where did you get yours?"

"Amarillo, Texas," I said.

Of course we went on with the conversation. She and her husband, a drama critic, were on their way to London, stopping off in New York to see what Broadway had to offer.

"What do you think of this play?" she asked me.

"What do you think?" I hedged.

"I think . . ." the words came out in a great rush. "I think if this is your best, God pity your worst!"

I told her I quite agreed with her, and we fell into a discussion of the reasons back of our judgment. I considered them valid and well taken at the time. I still do.

"What was his purpose in writing it?" she asked, just as the lights blinked, warning us it was time to go back to our seats. "What was he trying to prove?"

I said I didn't know. I still don't. The burden of the play seemed to be the complaint of a young man who felt he was the victim of a world he never made. So what. Nobody ever made the world in which he lived, going back to the first man to inhabit it. Granted that the world is beset by problems and the people in it are troubled and disturbed, with good reason. That is the theme of some of the greatest literature—the struggle and the endurance of mankind. In his very struggle is a kind of glory.

When I was little, or so I am told, I was given to breaking things—my dolls, my toy dishes, even, upon occasion, my own small bones. At such times I would interrupt my wails to say, "Papa'll fix it!"

Usually he could.

That is the great cry now—for someone to fix things. Parents. Teachers. Committees. Legislation. Any housewife could tell the people making these demands that the day of the general handyman is over. Best they learn to do a bit of tinkering on their own.

A story is told of a young man shaking his fist at heaven and crying out, "Lord, what an awful world this is! I could have made a better one myself."

A voice from above answered him. "That's why I sent you there. Get busy."

I would like to think the young man thus admonished did get busy, because that is the sort of person I admire. One who will try to correct a wrong rather than merely bewail it. For that reason I undertook the writing of *Many A Voyage,* the book about Edmund Ross, the Kansas senator whose single vote is commonly given credit for the acquittal of President Johnson at his impeachment trial and thus, according to reliable students of history, saving the constitutional form of government for the United States. Here was a man willing to do something about his convictions.

The idea was first suggested to me in 1955 by Mr. Bond, who had read a fleeting reference to the Senator in an account of the trial. In recent years so much publicity has been given to Ross and his vote that it is difficult to realize I had never before heard of the man. At the time I felt no wish to undertake the proposed book. I did, however, agree to consider the matter, but when I returned to Texas I had to push any thought of a book into the background, taking time out to move to Amarillo. I rented the same house I had once shared with my friend, the place where I had read proof on my first book, *Separate Star,* had set down a few tentative ideas for *Fair Is the Morning,* and had run across a phrase I tucked away in my mind, thinking some day I would use it as a title of a book. It was *The Years of the Locust.*

Came moving day. I watched the transfer people leave with the last load and for a little while I stood in the empty house, remembering things that had happened in the years I had lived here. It would always be a part of me, that I knew. Perhaps, in a way, I would be a part of it. Somewhere in those beamed ceilings a certain essence might linger. Perhaps footprints those oak floors had known would stay, just a little. Only a short while I stood there in the empty silence, and then I walked out, closing the door behind me for the last time.

I knew it was not just a house I was leaving, but a way of life as well.

By this time I was teaching only creative writing, with a special and interesting addition to the regular class work. In 1952, with the backing of President James Cornette and of Dr. A. Kirk Knott, head of the English department, our school had started the practice of allowing a candidate for a Master's Degree in English, if he so desired, to write a creative thesis. It was my happy privilege to supervise these theses. Some excellent material has resulted. Books, both fiction and nonfiction. Plays, both originals and adaptations of well-known books or short stories. Influenced by the quality and success of these creative theses, several other departments in our school have used the same plan.

Presently, my teaching assignment consists of only one advanced class, offered one semester each year. The members of the group, however, are always so deeply immersed in their projects that they continue meeting every week, summer and winter, whether I am teaching or not. I have a most excellent substitute who presides at meetings I am unable to attend.

The first few sessions of the new semester are held on the campus. After that students gather at my house or in the homes of the various members. Officially, the hours are from seven until nine-thirty. Actually, class members begin arriving as early as six-thirty, and a few have been known to stay until nearly midnight.

There are refreshments of the simplest sort—coffee, soft drinks, a few things for nibbling. Members read their own material, with everyone sitting on the edge of his chair, taking notes, listening, ready to give criticism and suggestions once the reader had finished.

"Do you know what I think about this class?" a young man asked.

The group was meeting at my house. A wood fire burned in the grate; the good smell of coffee filled the air. I braced myself for his evaluation. He was an excellent student, having attended several universities, including some in Europe. Perhaps he would consider this group a sort of club, gathered for no purpose beyond food and fun.

"What?" I asked.

"It is my idea of what a university class, in the real sense of the word, should be," he told me. "It's like the old English coffee houses. Samuel Johnson, and that sort of thing."

To me it is more than that. Louis Pasteur admonishes scientists against living apart from the world "in the serene peace of laboratories." I did not live apart, and in my very involvement I think my life gained an added dimension, both as a writer and as a teacher. And perhaps in still another way, as expressed by a young student.

"I sometimes wonder if I could have been a much better writer had I quit teaching and done nothing but write," I said. This had been a trying day, with many interruptions. And now, the class.

"Oh, don't say that," the young student protested. "This way you are—" he hesitated, evidently groping for the right words, then brought them out triumphantly, "This way you are *a part of people!*"

Oh, I was all right. As a result I could understand most of the difficulties which might beset the members of my class. A crowded schedule? That I knew full well. Interruptions? Those I had in full measure. I shared their difficulty in making words do one's bidding, of trying to reconcile the beautiful thought with the prosaic way one is finally able to set it down on paper. I had full knowledge of how a wonderful idea can be lost before it is ever written, all because the telephone rang at the wrong time.

But there are compensations. Your joints may begin to creak a little and your hair require a rinse with a poetic name, but the spirit—oh, it remains the younger for being able to associate with young people. This matter of youth among the students is not always chronological. One of the youngest minds I have ever had in my classes belonged to a woman in her eighties. Youth may be a thing of the spirit, generated by an idea.

It is an experience that grows and enlarges with the passing of time. They keep up with me, those students of mine. In Lima, Peru, I had lunch with a young man who had once been in my class. His wife met me at my hotel and took me to their home. Former students popped up all over Europe during the months I was there. When I deplaned in Honolulu, one of them was waiting for me, an orchid *lei* in his hands. New York is a place of many happy reunions, for of course young people interested in writing have a tendency to find their way there. It is my firm conviction that, should I take the first spaceship to the moon, a young man, already there, will walk up to me and say, "Remember me, Miss Erdman? You used to teach me."

Letters from former students bring news of themselves. Books or stories they themselves have sold. New jobs. Promotions. Engagements. Weddings. Babies. Upon occasion I have played an active part in some of these happy activities. Once I acted as mother of the bride when the girl's mother was unable to attend the ceremony; I played the same role for a young groom whose mother could not come to the wedding. I have godchildren and namesakes. I think Mr. Pasteur would approve of me. He could never accuse me of retiring to the serene peace of a library, apart from real people. Actually, my experience had prepared me for a study of Edmund Ross, a man who spent his life in the middle of activity.

Already I knew from having written regional books such as *The Edge of Time* and my historical novel. *The Short Summer,* the importance of going to primary sources for information. Had I read only the brief and fleeting references to Ross in the material which started me on my project (or had I been content with the current and popular notion about the man) I would have pictured him as a nobody who came out of obscurity to cast his deciding vote and, once this was finished, crept back into obscurity again. Nothing could be farther from the truth. He put his mark on every region in which he lived—Ohio, Milwaukee, Kansas, New Mexico. And of course, on the entire nation because of his vote.

I reasoned that, since he was a Kansas senator at the time of the impeachment trial, the obvious place to start my investigations would be the Kansas State Historical Museum in Topeka. Museums—local, regional, state—can open up vast stores of information for anyone who wants to write an historical or regional book. The staff members are in themselves walking encyclopedias concerning the material the writer needs. Certainly I found this to be true in Topeka.

Here I found the record of Ross's career in Kansas. Had he never gone beyond that, he would have been worthy of consideration. He came with one of the first groups to make their way across the Lane Trail (named after James Lane, the ill-starred Kansas senator whose place Ross was later to take) in the interest of making Kansas a Free State. Once in Topeka, Ross and his brother published a newspaper filled with Free State editorials and with other items calculated to further the interests of the then-Territory of Kansas. He helped write the constitution under which Kansas was admitted to the Union. The original document, with Ross's name signed to it, is in the museum at Topeka.

He was much involved in politics, a stormy business in those years before the Civil War when Missourians and Kansans were literally at each others' throats. It is a mistake to assume, as many people do, that the Civil War was fought entirely in the Middle and Southern States. Much fighting took place on the Western Border. Some students of history maintain the Civil War began on the Missouri-Kansas Border long before Fort Sumter. The phrase, "Poor Bleeding Kansas," was used as a rallying cry even before Lincoln's nomination for his first term as president. Lincoln spoke in Leavenworth, Kansas, in December 1859. (I read the account in the Leavenworth *Times*.) Later he gave the essence of this same speech, his House Divided one, at Cooper Union and, partly because of it, was nominated.

Edmund Ross worked hard to bring the Santa Fe Railroad into being. I read his editorials advancing its cause. He gave it the name it bears, dug the first shovel of dirt and delivered the main speech at its dedication in Topeka in October 1868.

He urged the adoption of a definite, constructive Indian policy and was sent as a member of a Congressional Committee to the Medicine Lodge Peace Conference. I read his report of the meeting as printed in the Lawrence (Kansas) *Journal*. I also read the stories of the event as written by another newsman for the St. Louis *Missouri Democrat*. A young reporter named Henry M. Stanley who is much better known for his immortal words, "Dr. Livingstone, I presume?"

As senator from Kansas, Ross was the first one to sign his name to the Commission given to Vinnie Ream, allowing her to do the statue of Lincoln now in the rotunda in the Capitol. (This information I found in the Library of Congress.) He had known the Reams in Kansas before they came to Washington; once here, Mrs. Ream ran a boardinghouse where Senator Ross stayed.

After the trial and his defeat for another term as Republican senator from Kansas, Ross ran for governor on the Democratic ticket and made not too bad a showing in that hitherto all Republican state. Again, I found this information in the museum.

I found other, more personal items there. Ross's own story of his life, written in his fine, steel-engraving script. And something else which gave added depth and meaning to the man and his family—letters he wrote to Fannie, his wife. While he was in the army. When he was in Washington. When he later went to New Mexico.

I wanted to know about his New Mexico career also, so naturally I went to the New Mexico Historical Museum in Santa Fe to do research there. I found that not only had he been territorial governor, living in the Old Palace, at that time used as the residence of the governor, but he also was the one who suggested it be used as a museum, a suggestion which was later carried out. He was instrumental in seeing that the Indian outlaw, Geronimo, ceased to scourge the lonely settlers trying to gain a foothold on the edge of civilization. He preached the doctrine of water conservation and the advantages of breeding better livestock. He worked for woman suffrage and for statehood. His record in New Mexico was an enviable one, but not untouched by conflict, since he was a man of strong convictions, always finding some cause to fight for.

Another source not to be overlooked by anyone wishing to write about history is the public library and the librarians who staff it. Naturally, I turned to these helpful people in Amarillo. They became so interested in my project that they sometimes ran ahead of me in my research. They also opened up for me the fascinating world of inter-library loan, a service of which I had known almost nothing. By this means I was able to obtain books not in our library, ones which were of great help to me. The public library of Milwaukee, Wisconsin, made it possible for me to have a look at rare manuscripts, books, and newspaper clippings. From these sources I was able to reconstruct Ross's life in Milwaukee.

Here, too, he had been prominent in the activities of the town. As a reporter on *The Free Democrat,* he wrote anti-slavary editorials which were widely read. He helped free Joshua Glover, an escaped slave, from a Milwaukee jail where he was being held until his Missouri owner could come for him, an act which set Wisconsin on a path that led it to defy the Supreme Court of the United States. In the library I found an account of the meeting at which Ross volunteered to go to Kansas "To give myself, my wife, and my three small children to the cause of Kansas."

In the Kansas City Public Library I came across a copy of an interview with Lillie Ross in which she gave details of the day the news of her father's vote came to Lawrence, Kansas, where the family lived. At a library in New York City, I read the newspapers giving accounts of the impeachment trial. There was not one sympathetic sentence about Ross in any of these.

I always try to visit the setting of my story and, if possible, talk with family, friends, or acquaintances of my main character. I was fortunate in being able to visit with members of the Ross family in Albuquerque; I exchanged letters with other relatives in various parts of the country. I find I can add authority and authenticity to my writing in this way, two qualities I prize. It was like a conversation I overheard between my grandniece (and namesake), Lou Anne, aged four, and her small brother, Robert Karl. He was too young to understand what she was saying, being less than a year old, but still she felt it necessary to explain to him that she had learned to print her name, an activity in which, at first try, she failed. Now that she had succeeded, she was describing the process.

"I have learned to write my name," she told him. "First I did it crooked but now I can write it straight."

I wanted to write this book straight.

A word of warning, though, to all who have the same wish about the books they write. Check and recheck all your information. Even primary sources can, upon occasion, be wrong. I found errors in family records, census reports, and newspaper stories. For instance, a news account has Ross say in his speech of vindication before the Senate, "I have taken *many a voyage* in the cause of right." I was so intrigued with the phrase that I used it as my title. Some instinct moved me to check more carefully, so I wrote the Library of Congress, asking for a copy of the speech. It came, and I found that what Ross really said was, "I have faced many a danger in the cause of right." By this time, however, I was so pleased with my proposed title that I retained it, putting the words into Fannie's thoughts.

Even with the most careful checking a writer may run into difficulty, especially if the book deals with an era which is long past. People will confuse the region as it is now with the way it was at the time the story took place, and some of them will maintain your information is incorrect. Another point to remember—the recollections of old-timers are not always as accurate as one could wish. But the spirit is there, the feel. Capture that and hold fast and comfort yourself that you are writing fiction, not an historical document. Certainly no writer can be excused for doing violence to established facts, but even so, he will find it difficult to prevent errors from creeping in at times.

Flaubert says that if you have a determined purpose, you are often aided by chance. He is very right. How else can I explain something which influenced the whole texture of my book.

I had gone to Topeka to do research and was spending the night at a hotel there. After dinner, I went into the lounge to watch a television program in progress. The man appearing was former Senator Henry Ashurst of Arizona. Only that day I had read a small item to the effect that one of the last people outside the family to talk with Edmund Ross was a then-young newspaper reporter named Henry Ashurst. He later became Senator from Arizona, the same man who now appeared on the screen before me. Just as I was making up my mind that I would write the old gentleman asking for information about the interview, I heard him say that he wished to thank all the friends and well-wishers for the thousands of letters that had been coming to him, but he knew they would understand when he told them he could not answer them. It so happened that I knew one of the young men who had some part in the televising of the program. I wrote him, explaining my problem. He showed the letter to the old Senator who penciled a few words across it, saying that if I came to Washington he would see me.

I went. Until now I had thought of Ross as a bedeviled, despised, downtrodden man. Senator Ashurst gave me a different picture.

"Don't make him an old sorehead, feeling the world was

against him," the Senator cautioned. "Ross was an intelligent, well-educated man, with a deep sense of responsibility. He was courteous and well groomed. In fact, he was a thoroughgoing gentleman."

We talked at some length about Edmund Ross. How he looked beyond his time, seeking better answers than those commonly accepted at the moment. I went away from the conference feeling that I could now take a fresh approach to my research. Ross was not a man who stepped briefly into the limelight and then disappeared; a nobody, who cast a vote and then dropped out of sight. Rather, he was a timeless, universal man who had a sense of responsibility and did something about his convictions. His was not the bitterness of idealistic youth, disillusioned because wrongs were not corrected immediately, once attention was called to them. He was a mature man pointing out existing problems, suggesting reasonable solutions, and then trying to act upon his own recommendations. And Fannie, with her ability to understand and appreciate him, was a fine strong woman in her own right.

Now I was sure of something that had been in the back of my mind for some time. I would write the book from Fannie Ross's point of view. This, although I had been able to find only three recorded facts about her—the day of her birth, the day of her marriage, the day of her death. No matter, I was all the more free to reconstruct her as I believed her to be. After all, I had read Ross's account of his life, which of course contained information about her. I had read the letters he wrote her; they were a mirror in which I could see her reflected through his eyes. She followed her husband wherever he went, either in body or spirit; she had said of him, "He would do right though the heavens fall." Ross was a man of strong convictions, each one a cause to fight for. He reached beyond his time, and so became timeless. It would take a very special kind of woman to appreciate and understand him. Such a woman I believed Fannie Lathrop Ross to be. A woman of courage, of intelligence, of charm. I gained additional details about her from the grandson in Albuquerque, including a picture of her and Edmund. True, it was taken when they were in their sixties, but even so, with the things he had told me about her, I was able to imagine what she was like.

It seems to me that, all things being equal, it is better for a woman writer to use a woman's point of view. Occasionally a critic or reviewer will say, "She writes like a woman," about a woman author of a current book. Why not? She is a woman and when did good writing come as a result of denying your own identity? Besides, what's wrong with woman writers? George Sand and George Eliot did not do so badly; nor did the Brontës or Willa Cather or Elizabeth Barrett Browning. Harriet Beecher Stowe was given credit by Lincoln for starting the Civil War and Ida Tarbell initiated some pretty good battles of her own. Writing like a woman is not an automatic indictment any more than writing like a man is a badge of quality. However, in this book I did not find my real difficulty lay in being a woman who was writing about a man, but, rather, something that came out of my own background.

I had grown up in western Missouri where the trouble between my own region and Kansas during and preceding the Civil War was still fresh in the minds of people who had the story passed on to them by parents and grandparents. I had heard many stories from my own grandparents on both sides of the house. None of these even hinted that Missourians did not fly around adjusting their halos during that difficult time. It was necessary for me to recheck information I had always taken for granted. Gaining a perspective, as it were. Seeing history not as a series of dates, of movements, of battles won or lost, but, rather, as people and the way they were affected by these happenings.

More than that—I must go beyond the region and see this story as it was—a drama set against a national backdrop. No region, no problem, is truly isolated. The things that happen in the most remote reaches of a land can, and often do, eventually become the concern of the nation. And perhaps, even the world. In the fifty years touched upon, Edmund Ross and Fannie, through his eyes, were both involved in one way or another with most of the great events of the period as well as the people who were a part of them. If ever there was a book where name dropping was indicated, this was it.

Carlyle, in "The Hero As a Man of Letters," says something about "One Life—a little gleam of time between two eternities." I would like to think I caught the gleam that was Edmund Ross and put him down clear and straight.

Many A Voyage was published in the fall of 1960. One of my clearest memories of the occasion was watching my mother as she listened to a review of the book. On her face was the polite, slightly puzzled expression of one who wants to understand but is having difficulty reconciling her own ideas with the version now being presented by a highly respected and unimpeachable source. This was certainly not the way she had heard the stories of the Border Warfare.

Still, it was my book and she would not—openly, at least—take issue with me. I devoted more attention to her than I did to the reviewer's comments.

In 1961, Kansas celebrated the centennial of her admission to the Union. As a gesture of recognition, the Kansas City *Star* ran *Many A Voyage* as a serial, the last one to appear in the paper. If the ship had to go down, I am glad I was on board.

In the fall of that same year, the Kansas State Librarians asked me to speak at their meeting in Topeka, using the book as the basis for my talk. Remembering the look on my mother's face as she had listened to the review, I chose the title, "That's Not the Way I Heard It!" giving some of my findings and pointing out how they differed from the stories I had heard when I was growing up. I told them of my mother's reactions and it was almost as if she were with me.

Only she wasn't. Shortly after the publication of *Many A Voyage* I went to New York for a month. My mother stayed with my sister while I was gone. Once I was home, Mama and I went back to our house. We unpacked and she settled herself in her own room with its familiar furnishings, the things she had brought from Missouri, the ones she had known all her married life.

"I'm glad to be back home," she said. "I sleep better, here in my own room, in my own bed."

And I said, "I sleep better, too, knowing you are here."

I told her good-night and went to my room.

She did not waken the next morning. She had, indeed, gone to sleep sometime during the night. Quietly. Apparently without pain or struggle. I myself found her when I went to her room to tell her breakfast was ready.

We took her back to Missouri for a service in the small church of which our family had been a part for so many years. Afterwards she was placed beside our father in the cemetery on the hill overlooking the town. And there we left them, surrounded by relatives and friends, as they had been in life.

It was a homecoming of sorts. Quite as she would have had it.

Chapter Eleven

Back in Texas, my sister and I did the necessary things, going through Mama's belongings, finding it in our hearts to wonder (as I am sure someone else will wonder when the time comes to perform a like service for us) why certain things are cherished and kept through the years. Feeling a tender sadness and, also, a certain steadying soberness that comes with realizing you are the first generation.

By and by this reorganization, both physical and emotional, was accomplished, and we went back to our regular routines. I thought it might be well to go through my own files, sorting, discarding, rearranging. In the process I came across a manuscript which I had discarded, feeling it had no promise. Now I decided that I might be able to make something out of it. With Lilian Kastendike's help I rewrote it as a novelette which eventually appeared in *Redbook*. It centered in a stranger who appears in a small Texas town, apparently finding it unnecessary to give any information about his own background but insisting that all the people around him be absolutely honest about themselves. The resulting complications set the town on its ears.

Later this novelette formed the lead (and title story) of a collection brought out by Dodd, Mead, *The Man Who Told the Truth*. It was well received, thus presenting another of the many arguments in favor of keeping one's files in order and occasionally taking stock. Sometimes a manuscript at first considered hopeless can be revised successfully. Perhaps any piece of writing is like a fruitcake—all the better for having been put aside for a while.

In going through my files I had found some information which illustrated how often writers can overlook material close at hand, thinking to find glamour in a distant landscape. This consisted of a brief reference to a group of French people who had settled in the Panhandle. I had filed it away with the notation that I should investigate the story. I turned to this now as possible material for a young people's book. Since I was going to Montreal anyway that summer, I thought it logical to make a side trip to Quebec which, to me, seemed the heart of the French influence in this continent. I did find material there, but nothing so valuable as the discovery that my best information was located in New Orleans.

I went to New Orleans and did indeed find much that was of the greatest help. I read newspapers. I talked with people old enough to remember the town as it was when my French family would have landed there. I haunted museums and walked the narrow, crooked streets. I soaked in atmosphere.

I found from reading the papers that President McKinley and his party visited New Orleans a short time before his assassination. I thought it would be rather a good touch to have my French family land in New Orleans in time to see the President, thus giving the children a sense of drama in the country of their adoption. By a fortunate set of circumstances I was able to talk with an older woman who as a child had watched the Presidential parade. Said she, "When President McKinley passed by, I was standing in the very front row of the crowd. He waved and smiled and it seemed that he looked only at me, that his smile was for me alone. A great man, President McKinley."

I used her experience in the book.

Back in the Panhandle, I continued my research, going through the same routine of reading in the library, visiting the site of the first French settlement here. I even talked with an older woman who as a child had been a part of it.

Eventually, *Room to Grow* was published, a book for young people, telling about a French family who settled in the Panhandle of Texas.

The files were destined to result in another book, one that came about almost by accident.

I had written a number of articles from time to time about my growing up in Missouri. They concerned school and church; the band concert in the park; the Sunday school picnic; family reunions and the annual Chautauqua. These were published in various magazines. After the Chautauqua one appeared I had a letter from an editor, one who evidently did not know my connection with my other two publishers, suggesting that I do a book of Americana incorporating this article. Of course I declined, explaining my reason. I found the publisher's letter when I was setting my files in order and just happened to mention it to Mr. Bond. Whereupon, he said Dodd, Mead would like for me to write that book for them. Accordingly, I began compiling the articles.

I changed a bit here and there; I made necessary transitions. I combined several and wrote a few new ones. But essentially, the material remained much as I had written it in the original versions. The book appeared under the title *Life Was Simpler Then*. I dedicated it to my brother and my sister who had lived these days along with me and, also, to the rest of the kin who will, I hope, say, "Yes, that's exactly the way it was."

Which is exactly what they have said. I prize their letters with their comments. Much better that they should feel as they did instead of saying, "Now didn't she make up a bunch of lies just to have a book."

One cousin said, "It was as if you had a tape recorder and a movie camera trained on us."

"Do you suppose it was all as wonderful as we remember it?" another cousin mused.

I said no, of course it wasn't. That is the magic of it all. Within our hearts we have built up our own oases of memories and from them we can draw refreshment. The actuality was transient and fleeting; the memory is something that lives forever. For here is America in essence. A region, a way of life recaptured. Not only for me and for my family, but for others as well. I continue to receive mail about this book, both from this country and from abroad. A teen-ager wrote from Germany:

"I have just finished reading your book *Life Was Simpler Then*. I am of a different age and a different country from you but I understood and enjoyed every word you wrote. Except—which side was William Jennings Bryan on?"

Try explaining the Scopes trial to a young German girl of today, especially when you yourself understood little about it when it was in progress except that your grandfather was all for Bryan.

I continue to receive many letters about the book from people of all ages, from all over the world. Each one who writes seems to feel, either from experience or intuition, that here is a valid and true slice of life as it was really lived. A segment of time recaptured—an era preserved for posterity. Perhaps, even, a type of artifact. Or something to be placed in a time capsule or buried in a cornerstone as being typical of the people who lived at the time.

Reading these letters I find myself wishing, as Horace expressed it in one of his odes, that "I might perhaps leave something so written they should not willingly let it die."

Or an even better wish—that it should be so written it would keep itself alive.

For a time after *Life Was Simpler Then* was published, I did no writing at all. This period of inactivity was broken by a suggestion from Mr. Bond.

"Why don't you write a book about Order Number Eleven?" he asked.

He was referring to the Military Order given by General Thomas Ewing, the Union general, after Quantrill's raid on Lawrence, Kansas, in August 1863. It affected the people in three and part of a fourth county in western Missouri, displacing somewhere between twenty and thirty thousand people, laying waste a stretch of land one hundred miles long and approximately thirty miles wide.

"Everybody already knows about that," I objected.

What I really meant was that everybody in Missouri knew about it, but with that touch of provincialism we never quite lose, I assumed the knowledge was general.

"On the contrary, nobody knows about it—except," he added quickly, doubtless moved by the look on my face, "except the people in western Missouri. Even few history buffs of that period. I've checked."

"Then how did you know?" I asked.

"Because you've mentioned it in every book you've written about Missouri."

"But it's a Civil War story, and people have had quite enough of them." I was still doubtful.

"No, it's a story of displaced people. It would be difficult to find a more contemporary theme than that."

He was right. The story of exiles making their weary way from refuge to refuge was as current as this morning's newspaper. Even so, I could not give up without more protest.

"But it's so drab," I said. "I mean—all their trouble and suffering—their homes burned and looted; their stock stolen; their fields laid waste."

My inherited anger rose, just to contemplate the event.

"Courage is never drab," he said simply. "And that, apparently, they had in full measure."

I promised to think it over and on that note I went back to Texas. Once I was there, I did turn my mind toward this Missouri book.

I had grown up on stories of Order Number 11. In our home, as well as in the homes of many of our friends, was a copy of the novel by that name, well worn from having been read by several generations. The book, however, gave little space to the actual order, dealing, rather, with the way of life of that period. We all were familiar with Bingham's picture of the same name. Originally it was titled "Martial Law," but later was known as "Order Number 11," since it depicted the eviction of a family during the enforcement of the order. It now hangs in the Historical Museum at Columbia, Missouri, and was on display in the Missouri Building at New York's 1964 World's Fair. Stories of the sufferings of the people displaced were part of the folk wisdom handed down by older generations. I began my reading with the smug complacency of someone who feels he already knows the subject at hand. The information I discovered was a revelation to me.

Missouri was, according to the authorities, one of the most sorely beset states in either the Union or the Confederacy. Here was fought Civil War in the truest sense of the word. At the war's beginning more than three-fourths of the people either had been born in slave states or were descended from parents who were. Yet many of the influential men of the state, slaveholders themselves, did not believe Missouri's future lay with the Confederacy. On the day Jefferson Davis was inaugurated as President of the Confederacy, Missourians voted almost 4 to 1 against secession. At the same time, they voted against Lincoln but elected as their governor Clairborne Jackson, a secret secessionist. In October 1861 the new governor summoned the state legislature to a meeting at Neosho in order to pass an ordinance of secession. In November, Jefferson Davis accepted Missouri as the twelfth state of the Confederacy.

A state convention met in Jefferson City, the capital, and, over the protest of some of its members, declared the offices of governor and lieutenant governor vacant, choosing Hamilton Gamble (himself born in the South) provisional governor. From that time on until the close of the Civil War, Missouri had two governments—the elected one locating after Jackson's death in Marshall, Texas, and also a provisional one headed by Gamble, sitting in Jefferson City.

To complicate matters further, General Frémont, from his headquarters in St. Louis, placed Missouri under martial law almost at the war's beginning, telling the Union Army to "live off the country." It was an order he did not see fit to change even after Lincoln himself questioned the wisdom of the move. Newspapers were forbidden to publish any news contrary to the wishes of the Union commanders. Some editors who defied the ruling had their buildings burned, their presses thrown into the Missouri River. Laws was administered by a system of provost marshals, themselves often corrupt and unscrupulous. Frémont also issued a decree freeing the slaves in Missouri before Lincoln got around to making his own proclamation.

And constantly there were raids made into Missouri by groups from Kansas—Redlegs, Jayhawkers, and, most despised of all, Jim Lane's men—who came across the border to loot and burn and steal.

A strange and contradictory people, these Missourians. Southern men, like Bingham the painter and Gamble the provisional governor, taking the oath of allegiance to the Union. Little Joe Shelby, the fiery Confederate general, refusing to surrender to the Union and instead, marching with some of his men down to Mexico to support Maximilian. Quantrill, the ne'er-do-well, neither Missourian nor Kansan, but drifting back and forth across the line, posing as the friend of both. He headed a vigilante group organized, or so he said, to protect Missouri from Kansas raiders. Later they became outlaws of the worst type.

Missouri, seeing herself as a transplanted southern society, yet designated as Mother of the West. Lovely pillared mansions and mountain cabins in the Ozarks. People whose ancestors went back far into the history of the nation living side by side with newcomers from many lands. She was the Missouri Compromise; she was Daniel Boone in a coonskin cap. She was metropolitan and rural; she was industrial and agricultural. She harvested cotton in the extreme south and ice in the middle and northern portions. She was, really, two states divided by The River. In Missouri many people still say The River, meaning the Missouri, and The War meaning the Civil War. There have been some upstart wars since, but they have names or numbers. The Civil War remains, quite simply, The War.

A great contradiction, the state of Missouri. Of mixed interests and ancestry. No wonder her symbol is the mule.

Even though I had grown up in Missouri—perhaps for this very reason—I knew I must go back, must have another look at the region and the information I had so long taken for granted. My first trip was to the State Historical Museum at Columbia, Missouri. The people in charge helped me locate much valuable material. Perhaps the most significant fact I learned was that the logical place to carry on my research would be in Jackson County, which had been in the middle of the distressed area. Accordingly I went to the Jackson County Historical Society files, housed in the Truman Library at Independence, Missouri. Here I struck pay dirt. In this museum are housed the memoirs, the letters, the interviews of people who themselves were either a part of the great exodus or whose ancestors were involved. Gradually I began to piece together the details of Order Number 11— not only the evacuation alone, but, also, the background for it and the far reaching chain of events which followed.

I drove over the roads these refugees had traveled. I knew, from pictures, or accounts, or buildings actually still standing, the sort of places in which they had taken refuge. I went to Lexington, county seat of my own home county, Lafayette, and saw there the famous old Anderson House, reconstructed as it had been when it was first built, having much of the same furniture, or at least pieces used during that period. I went through the Wornall House in Kansas City and the Old Jail in Independence. Slowly the people in my story began to come alive, as did the region in which they lived and the events which had happened.

I was beginning to see something I had not realized was possible. The work I had done in my research for *Many A Voyage* was helping me now. Not in the information gained, although that was not to be discounted. But in another, more subtle way. Kipling said, "What should they know of England who only England know!" As far as that goes, what should they know of teaching who only teaching know? Or writing? Or any other way of life of which only one angle is clear. Having seen the Kansas side of The Late Unpleasantness, I could see now, more clearly and with greater understanding, the things which happened in Missouri. It gave a certain remoteness, a certain ability to judge.

There was another, an even greater gain. In my other Missouri books I had told about a way of life I knew so well, the essence that was me. Now I was going deeper. I was understanding—dimly at first, but a little more clearly as I went on—why we were as we were. What do you know of your own background if that is all you know?

A good trick if you can manage it, this business of knowing one's self.

I remember quite well the story my mother told about her first meeting with my father (who, of course, wasn't anybody's father at the time). She was visiting her grandmother and an uncle brought a young man in to meet her, one he felt was extremely eligible. Mama, who was left-handed, was sewing when they came into the sitting room. She saw a tall young man with black slightly curly hair and blue eyes, who indicated quite plainly that he thought he was looking at a very pretty young girl, one he would like to impress. So what did he do? Certainly not the obvious or ordinary.

A week or so later a package came to my mother from a mail-order house. When she opened it, she found a pair of left-handed scissors. The way Mama told it, this was a gift more romantic than flowers or candy or a love song sung under her window. For it showed that here was a young man who had really noticed her and was anxious to do things which would add to her comfort. To cherish her, as the wedding ceremony so aptly put it. That's why, she said, she looked kindly upon his suit, favoring him over the other young men who were hanging around at the time.

With a child's literal mindedness, I assumed my mother's decision had come solely as a result of the gift and I was who I was—Loula Grace Erdman (named for an aunt because it was the custom in my father's family to pass the name down from aunt to niece)—all because of a pair of left-handed scissors. And I would wonder, with that shivering half-fear, half-pleasure that comes of contemplating danger when one

is quite safe, what would have happened had the order been
lost or filled incorrectly. Or, even worse, if my father had
not known there was such a thing as left-handed scissors.
But of course, since he was all wise and all powerful, he
would know about them as he knew about everything else.

The story came back to me now as I did my research, delv-
ing into the reasons underlying the story I wanted to tell.
Not just the *who* and the *what* of it, but the *why* as well.
And, perhaps also, the *what if's!* But most of all, the necessity
for looking into the many and complex reasons back of any
event.

I was getting these stories and anecdotes, setting down
events as I heard them, hoping to pass them on in permanent
form. That is the way much history has passed into literature.
The wandering minstrels went from castle to castle, relating
incidents they deemed worthy of retelling, celebrating heroes
and great deeds. They put their tales to music, no doubt
giving their own interpretations, adding drama and suspense,
bringing characters to life. Preserving something that otherwise might have been lost. Because of them, Homer had
material for his *Iliad* and *Odyssey;* Malory for *Morte
d'Arthur.*

That lantern business again. Now it was in my hands and
I was training the light on an episode of history scarcely
known outside the region where it had taken place. President
Truman, when asked by the historian, Samuel Eliot Morison,
to recommend a good history dealing with Missouri during
the Civil War, said, "There isn't one. They're all liars."

I talked with people whose grandparents had been a part
of the great exodus. I read their stories in letters and diaries.
At times, some of the information seemed to have little con-

nection with the subject I was exploring. It was like pieces
of a jigsaw puzzle spilled carelessly on the floor; if they were
to mean anything, I must put them together with order and
purpose. Not an easy task, this, for the pieces were both
various and complex. And some of them were of such nature
that I wondered why historians had paid so little attention to
them.

For instance, Order Number 11 ravaged a much larger
territory than did the Siege of Atlanta, affected more people.
So far as I was able to learn, the refugees displaced by this
order were the only ones in history who were merely told
to get out with no destination named. The Indians on the
Trail of Tears knew Oklahoma Territory would be their
stopping place; the Acadians were destined to settle in other
British colonies; the Israelites were headed for a Promised
Land with Moses to lead them. Order Number 11 evacuees
had neither leader nor place of refuge. They went as families;
they went as small units drawn together by chance or necessity; they went as individuals. Old and young, black and
white, rich and poor, sick and well—they moved along, without hope, without direction.

The conditions of the exodus were even more devastating
because the Order was enforced not by regular Union soldiers as would have been expected, but rather by members
of the Kansas State Militia, many of whom had personal
grievances against the people at whom the Order was directed. In some cases, former slaves came back to assist in
driving out their onetime masters.

Albert Castel, the Kansas historian, says, "Order Number
11 was the most drastic and repressive military measure
directed against civilians during the Civil War. In fact, with

the exception of the hysteria-motivated herding of Japanese-Americans into concentration camps during World War II, it stands as the harshest treatment ever imposed on United States citizens during our nation's history."

I had chosen to see the story through the eyes of three families, different in background and outlook but bound together by a common danger, a common need. They represented all displaced people, not only at this time but since the history of refugees began. Their courage and their dignity. Their kindness to others who needed help. Their weaknesses and strengths. Some of our finest books, our best plays, our most appealing movies have been based on the theme of displaced people. Here also was the bittersweet air that hangs over the death of a way of life. There is some quality within the human heart which makes us cling to the thing that is gone, to look back with sweet sadness on a landscape never to be revisited.

Certainly the book was not easy to write. Rarely did the writing go as I wanted it to, but I kept at it. I rewrote. I revised. I threw out the pages and started all over again. That is where writing has the edge on life—we can have a second chance. And a third. And more, if the need seems indicated. Finally, *Another Spring* was finished and off it went to the publishers. They set release date for October.

In April before publication I went back to my own home county, Lafayette (which, although not one of the counties evacuated by Order Number 11, still was touched by the suffering and upheaval), there to discuss the book before the Lafayette County Historical Society. Aunts and uncles gathered around; cousins and in-laws; friends and former schoolmates. It was a thoroughly rewarding experience.

The great experience was yet to come, however. *Another Spring* was launched in Kansas City at a Book and Author Dinner at the Muehlebach Hotel. To anyone growing up in my part of the state that represented the ultimate in elegance and distinction. Phelps Platt, now president of Dodd, Mead, came for the festivities, making me feel as if I had the special blessing of my publishers.

This was not my first time to speak in Kansas City. After the publication of *The Years of the Locust* I had addressed the Kansas City Pen Women. I had spoken as a native daughter (and a member of the organization) at a Theta Sigma Phi Matrix Table Dinner when the national convention was held in that city. But this was different. I was talking about a book set in this very region, one for which the people here had helped me gather material. They knew it for their own, and they approved. The Kansas City *Star* review had called it ". . . an outstanding historical novel of the tragic event known as Order Number 11 . . . the salient fact impressing this reviewer is its absolute historical accuracy."

Behind the platform as I spoke was a copy of Bingham's famous picture, "Order Number 11." Before me, in the audience, were relatives and friends, their hearts and minds reaching out not only to me but to the book I had written. There were other speakers on the program, naturally. Along with them, I had attended parties, had been presented with a key to the city. But in some beautiful way I could feel about it all—the decorations, the audience, the excitement, the applause—as the little girl in New Orleans had felt when she saw President McKinley. "It was all for me."

In spite of theories to the contrary, it is possible to go

home again, both in body and in spirit. I had done so, and forever after I could hold the memory of that homecoming in my heart, as I could hold in my hand the book, *Another Spring*, which had been the reason for it all.

And now, this book.

The suggestion that I write it was first made some fifteen years ago and half a world away. In the summer of 1953 while I was in England staying in the home of my British publisher and his wife, Paul and Felicity Hodder-Williams, we were having tea in the garden in a proper British fashion and I was telling an amusing incident connected with my writing.

"I say, Lou," Paul told me, "you should write a book about your writing experiences."

"Oh, that would be pretty small potatoes," I quipped, quoting the words of the neighbor at the time my first story was published.

We went on to talk of other things and in a few weeks I came home. In the months that followed I tried jotting down some of my writing experiences. Later, for various reasons, I discarded the idea.

I had quite forgotten about it when, in the fall of 1967, I was having lunch with Phelps Platt. I was in the process of telling an incident connected with the writing of *Another Spring*. He found it highly amusing.

"You should write a book about your writing experiences," he said.

Almost the identical words Paul Hodder-Williams had used. I told him this, without having any serious intention of following the suggestion he had made. The idea did stay with me, though, and when I went back to Texas I got out the old manuscript, yellowed with the passing of time. Still, I could not feel there was a book here.

I wonder if any writer ever really wants to start another book. I once heard an author say that she loathed writing; she loved *having* written. I am sure her sentiment is echoed by most writers. Yet there is apparently some lemminglike instinct that pushes us back to our typewriters regardless of how little we think we really want to go. Few indeed are the authors who quit with a single book to their credit, especially if the initial effort is a successful one. So few indeed that we always wonder why they did not write more.

I was at it again, nibbling around the edges of the idea, rejecting it, turning my thoughts instead to another book, one I had considered doing some years ago. Before I really got started on it, however, I found someone else was doing a book on the subject and dropped the idea. (Moral: If you have a plan for a book, get busy. Another writer is probably thinking about that same subject; he may even have made a start at writing it.) I rejected a second idea because it was the sort of project in which I had no wish to engage at the moment. (I may do it eventually—if somebody else doesn't beat me to it.)

With both of these tentative subjects out of the way, I now brought out the old manuscript, the one suggested by both my British and American publishers, and began looking at it once more. Perhaps I would really have started work on it without further encouragement, but actually I give credit to my students for pushing me on. They were meeting, as is their custom, during the summer. No credit, not really a class. Just keeping in practice, as it were.

They had gathered at my house one evening when someone asked casually how I had started writing. I hesitated a
moment, and then said I had written down an account of
my early experiences and if they were really interested, I
would read it to them. They said that was fine—after all, I
had not yet taken my customary turn. So I dragged out the
yellowed pages, cleared my throat, and began.

After I had finished, we all fell to discussing not only my
manuscript but this whole business of writing as well. I repeated the judgment of my nephew—that it was the great
wish of every human heart, the wish to communicate—and
they all agreed. One of them said, "By all means, continue
writing the book, if for no other reason than to give information about this universal wish."

After that, I felt more or less committed to the book.
I interrupted the writing, however, with a month's swing
around South America. In Bogota, Colombia, I visited an
English class taught by a cousin of mine in the University of
the Andes. Students from literally all over the world sat
listening as this young American teacher told them I wrote,
and even showed them a copy of *The Years of the Locust*.
The questions came thick and fast; the students were intensely interested in writing. That evening Pegi, the young
cousin, had a group of friend come to her apartment to meet
me, most of them writers themselves. Again, the questions,
the discussions, the talk of mutual problems in the writing
business. It was, apparently, the universal wish.

As I traveled, I jotted down ideas when they came—a line
or two in Lima; some good bits in Santiago; several pages
during the long ride from Rio to Miami. Back home, I once
more got out the pages I had written, considering how best

to approach this book. In fact, whether to approach it at all. I had been brought up to think it was poor taste to talk overmuch about myself. An entire book about me might be more than I, or anyone else, could face. Yet, no less authority than Gorky had said that everyone should write his autobiography.

For whose sake? His own, or others?

Certainly not for my own. But if it were true that so many people wanted to write, perhaps the experience of one writer might prove interesting and helpful as well. A sort of map, as it were, for those who wanted to travel the same road. Or even for those who, with no real desire to write, still would be interested in knowing something about it. The same spirit which turns the stay-at-home to books of travel and adventure. If I did it, I decided, I would use a rule-of-thumb test on every incident I included. It must be something which would be directly connected with my writing.

While I hesitated, Maurice Crain, my agent, came to Texas to visit his family. He read the portion I had finished and urged me to go ahead with it. He discussed the matter with Dodd, Mead once he was back in New York, and the word came that they, too, approved, especially Phelps Platt who had already suggested I write it.

And so I was off again, writing another book.

Much as one might want to do so, it is impossible to separate completely the writer from his writing. You are it and it is you. For if we really want to write, we must turn our eyes inward. On our own beliefs. Our motives. Our convictions. The philosophies that guide our lives. What is this wish to write, anyway? A perverse desire to move backward and forward at will in time and space, free from the laws

that govern ordinary human beings? Perhaps. Since the
World's beginning, man has sought freedom of body and
spirit, a desire immortalized in legend and story. Daedalus,
inventing wings in order that he and his son might escape
imprisonment; the Little Lame Prince, lifted above his in-
firmity; Scrooge, moving backward and forward in time;
Mary Poppins, the best of all, because she could take others
with her in her flights. Is that why writing is the great adventure—because it frees both writer and reader from their
human limitations?

Or does it go beyond that, in an instinctive reaching out
toward something larger, something better, something more
lasting than ourselves? A monument to a person, an idea, a
conviction. Because of something we have written, others
may take the wings of the morning and fly to the utmost ends
of the earth—or above, or around, or beneath it. And thus
we will have achieved immortality for ourselves.

In Ecclesiastes, the preacher tells us that to everything
there is a season and a time for every purpose under the sun.
He does not include writing, but perhaps he felt it was not
necessary to do so since he had already listed the great experiences of life, the ones with which most authors concern
themselves. Work and rest. Love and hate. Joy and sorrow.
Birth and death.

Or perhaps the preacher, being a very wise man, thought
it was not necessary to mention an obvious fact, one that
Dr. Johnson put into words centuries later. Said he, "A man
may write at any time if he sets himself doggedly to do it."

An awesome thing to contemplate, this writing business.
The Great Wish? The Great Escape? The Great Adventure?

The desire to become gods, creating beings whose destinies we may hold in our hands? Who knows for sure?

It may be just as well that a writer refrains from immersing himself too deeply in the philosophy back of it all, much less to discuss it at great length. Plato warned his wise men against deserting the world of practical affairs in favor of a life of contemplation; Caesar feared Cassius because he thought too much.

Better we writers go to our typewriters and get busy writing another book. Or, failing that, reading one that someone else has written. Perhaps somewhere in our writing, or our reading, we will find the answers to the questions we ask.